# Grief
## and
# Loss

## The Start ...
## we call the End

## Jim Gordon, Ph.D.
### Edited by Betty DeGeneres

**For Additional
Information and Books
Please
Visit my Websites:**

**BHCounseling.com
BeverlyHillsSelfHelp.com
JimGordonPhD.com** (books)

GriefAndLossBeverlyHills.com
emotional-incest.com

I met Dr. Jim Gordon when I bought a condo in the same building he lives in. At the time I was a Speech Pathologist in the Rehabilitation Dept. at Cedars-Sinai Medical Center, so I know all too well the subject of Grief and Loss. And when some of my family members died, Dr. Gordon sent me helpful, healing information and let me talk out my feelings with him. In this book, you'll read all sorts of practical advice. I've underlined some of my favorites - and I hope you will too.

Betty DeGeneres

Jim, When I got your book in the mail, I set it down with a bunch of other books to read. The other day, I came home from hospital, and was assigned Hospice care for 6 months due to 'old age' and failing organs. I picked up your book, and thought I'd peruse it, but I read it cover to cover. Oh my, it is so right on with what I feel. Thank you.

Harriet Pearl, teacher, 1920-2013

As one of the first 'lay' leaders of an Ecumenical Council of churches, I will always remember and appreciate your thrust in the 10 years you chaired – "Commonalities not Differences." Catholic, Jewish, and six Protestant Churches working together – your legacy.

Reverend John Parscouta

Jim, we go back years, you helped me with my 'AA Babies' so many times when they were diagnosed with AIDS, and you had the words for me to help them through their illness. I needed real words, not a script and you gave them to me.

Ernestine Mercer, actress, Young and the Restless

So many times at the hospital we had to share the final days or weeks with the patients. Thank you for your support. You were able to help them, and help me help them end their journey with dignity.

Randy N., nurse practitioner

ISBN-10: 1511518170/ ISBN-13:978-1511518178
5th Edition, COPYRIGHT 2024, Beverly Hills, CA.  ALL RIGHTS RESERVED.

**\*\*\*\*\*\*\*\***

Dear Reader:

   I wrote and compiled this book about Grief and Loss to help you get through the difficult time you are probably experiencing that brought you to read this.

   This book will help you make YOUR FUTURE a better and stronger place so that some day you can look back at this difficult time you are going through, and realize that even with a loss, you can take things with you that will help you move forward. Also, I hope to help you roll on with a better future, more strength, and more hope, for the rest of your Tomorrows!

   In a sense, Life Coaching is what we will be doing together throughout this book. It is about using what good tools you DO have, and moving forward with them versus dwelling on the past. Remember though that while this material can be therapeutic, it is NOT a substitute for Individual Counseling or Therapy, and/or Bereavement Groups.

   Yes, this IS a rough time for you, but you can grow from it. You will have a future, so hold on, and we shall work together through my book.

   And for the young folks I wish I could tell you that I have left you a perfect world when I die, but instead I have left some tools that help you do better with the Future. Not only do YOU have a FUTURE, but you ARE the FUTURE!  And now, let's talk and get through this Life together.

dr. g.

Dr. Jim Gordon
Beverly Hills, CA ©2024
BHCounseling.com / JimGordonPhD.com

**\*\*\*\*\*\*\*\***

This poem is from a very special Lady who was a true gentle soul, who touched many hearts during her lifetime... and certainly touched mine as we talked about Life.

## A POEM OF LIFE

A poem has a beginning,
a middle and an end.
It prepares us
for what is to come.
Holds our interest,
and lets us down gently.

Life has a beginning,
a middle and an end.
Are we ever prepared
for what is to come?
It surely holds our interest,
and as for the end, all we ask,
is that we be let down...
gently.

- Helen Currie -

# Table of Contents

Twin Towers Memorial Lights

# INTRODUCTION

## With Every GOOD BYE

After awhile you learn the subtle difference between
holding a hand and changing a soul,
And you learn that love doesn't mean leaning
and company doesn't mean security,
And you begin to learn that kisses aren't contracts,
and presents aren't promises.

And you begin to accept your defeats
with your head up and your eyes open,
With the strength of an adult,
not the grief of a child,
And learn to build all your roads on today
because tomorrow's ground is too uncertain for Plans,
And futures have a way of falling down in mid-flight.

After awhile you learn that even sunshine burns
if you get too much.
So plant your own garden
and decorate your own soul, instead of
Waiting for someone to bring you flowers.

And You Learn
That You Really Can Endure.
That You Are Really Strong,
and You Really Do Have Worth.

And You Learn and Learn
... With Every Goodbye,
You Learn.

## INTRODUCTION

In this book, you will find practical suggestions for getting through loss. There are quotes, poems, and stories. I believe there is little sense in 're-inventing' the wheel. Since man began, there have been losses from everything from fires to earthquakes to death. So much has been written about life-and-death over the years. Each religion and culture has its own definition of death, and the afterlife, however they view it.

Therefore, most everything presented in this book has been presented before, in some form or another. The commentary and editorializing is from me, along with some wisdom I've garnered. The rest of the wisdom is from others who've written, talked, and survived losses themselves.

Your survival and how to make peace with yourself, redefine your life and create the best future is our goal together. To help you find your best ways to get a better handle on your Life and take some of those Steps as you move forward from this difficult time.

Loss is usually equated with death, but the reality is that we suffer many types of losses in our lives. Those losses can include things such as the loss of innocence, as we grow up and realize there may truly not be a Santa Claus or a tooth fairy. It can be realizing that as we get older there are expectations made on us, such as getting a job, taking care of a family, and paying bills. For many people one of the first traumas is that loss of your first baby tooth. We have all seen children who get somewhat panicked, and maybe not just somewhat but totally panicked, when the first tooth falls out and parents try so hard to assuage the child that this is just part of their normal growth.

Children also tend to go through a period of time when they realize that the death that they have observed in their goldfish, hamsters, or other pets could also happen to mom and dad. Many a child has spent a traumatized night crying after experiencing the death of a pet, or a friend, and they want to be assured that mom and dad won't be dying now too.

In FULGHUM's "All I Need to Know I Learned in Kindergarten" he addresses this stark REALITY (the full poem is in the APPENDIX, check it out):

"Be aware of wonder. Remember the little seed in the . Styrofoam cup: The roots go down and the plant goes up and nobody really knows how or why, but we are all like that.

Goldfish and hamsters and white mice and even the little seed in that Styrofoam cup--they all die. So do we."

Remember, not all Loss is Death related. A major loss is the Loss of Innocence and Naivete. Such an occurrence is experienced by graduating from high school. For many kids, schooling - from pre-school to high school - is a time of camaraderie, spent with familiar friends who have grown up together, and now, for many, it means going off to a college in another part of the country, sometimes even another part of the world and meeting everybody new. Reality hits. Their  family and old friends are not there to hang out with. Sometimes, spending what should be the first exciting weekend at the new college dorm, or apartment near the college, can be very sobering. It's another way of cutting the umbilical cord, and forcing someone to grow.

Turning 18 in the USA, becoming adult is another eye opener. Oh my, so much can be written about that one!

Yes, it is an 'end' of an era in your life, but the 'start' of your Future.

This brings up a quick thought to share. In the 1970's, the phrase, "Today is the First Day of the Rest of Your Life" took off as the buzz phrase for a while. I remember seeing it on patches on jackets and shirts back then. It was attributed to the founder of Synanon, a drug re-hab program with a dubious record - BUT the thought is appropriate not just for folks who end drug use and re-start their lives but for all of us and particularly those recovering from a loss. What is behind us we can do little about changing, but... we can start to LIVE from here forward.

Along that line of thought, when I was thinking about titles for this book, and a college class I teach based on it, some titles that came to mind were:

"Open a new window, open a new door while saying Goodbye."
"Endings...that lead to Beginnings"
"Endings make room for Beginning anew"
"Ending one chapter, Beginning another"
"New Beginnings.... triggered by Endings"
"The Beginning, We call the END"

All have the same basic meaning - Move Forward at this Point, not Backward.

Talking about Loss and Endings always sounds so final, and finding a way to 're-frame' it is not easy.

5

Recognizing that there are so many new starts in our lives is one way of de-demonizing the word Loss.

Another 'living' related loss for many kids is that first time they realize that someone they trusted, cared about, and believed in as a friend - lied to them, or stole something from them. That Realization that everyone is not "nice" and forthright is a sobering loss of innocence issue. It does not have to make one cynical and rejecting of all humanity, but that loss pushes one further into Reality.

Life is an ongoing progression of losses. When one reaches their 20th birthday, and realizes their teenage years are over, that can be a big shock to the system. And we all know that the milestones of turning 30, 40, 50, and Medicare age, are also times of loss. As those times are reflected upon, as we look back, it is usually about what we have or haven't done, what we wished we would have done, and at some point in our lives, it is scary to realize that we have much less time in front of us than behind us. That type of reflection, adds a new urgency to accomplish things. There often is that shock at those milestones, and the realization that we are mortal. MORTAL. A scary thought. While accepting that we are still alive, we realize there is an end to this journey. Which is why some religions have coined the phrase, "the birth we call death". For many religions and beliefs, our time on earth is just a trial for the great afterlife, whether it be heaven, whether it be returning to Earth in a different form, or however it is defined by each belief and culture.

Ending a career may mean it's time for something new to happen for you. Ending a friendship with one person may mean the beginning of a friendship with somebody new, some wonderful new person who you might not have met had you stayed in your old rut.

Please realize that nobody is saying that you shouldn't feel bad about what happened, about your loss. Nobody is saying you don't have the right to lament and feel angst over the end of your relationship, your friendship, your job, or the death of someone close to you. What we are saying is what you do with it and how you handle it from here forward is what's going to be productive for you.

I truly believe that change often produces growth. An example now is our depressed economy, and this will probably be true for quite a few more years, it's not easy to make money. Many jobs and careers that were automatically paying comfortable incomes in the past, or had lots of security, are gone. But now that the economy's bad, people are having to work harder and more creatively, and have to think and sort things out. Money just doesn't 'flow' anymore.

One religion had a book years ago, called "the Birth, we call Death". Obviously the focus was towards death opening the door to heaven and eternal life. Well, no matter what your beliefs are, or what your faith is, the life you have now is the life you have – Now! Period. And what you have after death won't be the same after you pass on to whatever there is on the other side. So make your life NOW the best you can, and remember, if you suffered a loss through a death, that person who died, most likely would be telling you, "Live now kid!" not, "Mope and Suffer!"

And just because life is over, and a loved one has died, for the people left it behind doesn't mean that everything is done. That it's time to pack it in and become part of the Pre-Dead something that I talk about later, which is why we describe many retirement areas like Florida, Palm Springs and parts of Phoenix - as "God's Waiting Room"! Sadly, many folks DO take that attitude, that Life is over after their spouse or partner dies, and many friends die, and they just hang out stoically awaiting their demise. Better to Live 'til you Die!

One Ad Campaign a few years ago coined the phrase, "There's Plenty of Time to Rest when you are Dead." Good perspective.

Most of my life, I have looked at things intensely. I call myself 'intensely mellow'. An oxymoron yes, but if you know me, it fits. I like to enjoy and kick back, but I have a great depth and miss little that goes on. As I say in another book - "I was Never a little Boy" - I've always been fascinated in how people look at life, and as I experienced more death and loss, I learned more about life.

My great-grandfather, who was a Byzantine Catholic priest, came to the United States. In those days in Europe, priests of the Byzantine Catholic faith, or Greek Catholic, were allowed to marry. He came to the United States and served parishes in Pennsylvania and other places on the east coast. I'd heard a lot about Father John from relatives, but I wanted to get to know more about him and his religion. He died a few years before I was born. So, on one of my trips back east I grabbed my mother-in-law, Muff, and we hopped in the car and drove to Kingston, Pennsylvania where Father John served the parish in 1920 to 1924. I am not a practicing Catholic, I was not raised in the Faith, but I have been fascinated with church beliefs. We visited his old church there.

I learned some more about Life on that trip, and death too. The priest we met at the church was interesting, and intense. He took us inside the church and prefaced it with that fact that we would probably find the look of the interior of their church - its design, colors and decorations - a bit different than we're used to in other religion's churches.

He told us, "In our faith, we want people to be looking forward to the End. Not as much wanting to die, but not being afraid to die. We want them to live and enjoy their lives until they do die. Too many people spend a lot of time panicking and fearing death, worried about what death has in store for them and they don't Live while they're alive! So our church depicts death and heaven, as a glorious thing. We use a lot of Gold Leaf in our church when showing Heaven. You look at the alter, and the ceiling murals, they all show happy, smiling cherub-like angels awaiting your arrival. It gives people something to look forward to, not to dread."

The priest said that their presentation of heaven was for folks to see heaven in its glory and the afterlife as being gold-leafed and very positive. This way, they can relax and just lose themselves into an excitement and a belief that things are going to be wonderful later so their people could go on and enjoy their time now, and live for today.

Over the years, I have experienced many people

who are afraid to go to sleep at night fearing that they're going to die in their sleep. Being a doctor/therapist working with terminally ill patients for many years in different settings, I was well aware of this syndrome. I also run into it with some of my senior citizen friends and patients who don't really want to go to sleep or go to bed at night, because they're afraid that they will wake up dead. One young man I knew would stay up all night until the sun came up. He was afraid to go to sleep when it was dark because he was afraid he would not wake up. He said he was more comfortable going to sleep with daylight because of different energy.

Can 'Loss' ever not be a bad thing? Many times I talk to people who never expected to be in the career they ended up in because of loss.

I experienced it myself. In high school, I really had intended to go on into dentistry. The Vietnam War and some family issues both interfered and brought my pursuit of a career in dentistry to a halt. I was very depressed, on the edge of suicidal. I thought life is over if I can't go and do what I want to do.

I never expected to go into the field of psychology. It was one of three things I used to point out in high school that I never wanted to do - along with teaching and farming! And here I am teaching at a college now, too! I originally started teaching as a temporary job during the Vietnam War, that teaching job lasted 13 "temporary" years. Then I left teaching and went into practice as a therapist. I had not expected to ever go back into teaching. But, twenty-five years later, an

10

opportunity came up to teach at the university level, I took it and I love it. Not something I expected to do.

If the Vietnam War had not come along, if the family issues have not caused trauma and ended (note I said ENDED, stopped, killed) my impending career in dentistry, or had I gone into dentistry, who knows? Maybe I would've been happier, maybe I wouldn't have been. I don't know. But it was a new beginning to a new life for me. And one with few regrets.

Many times we get to a fork in the road where we have to make a decision. It's not quite an End, but it is a decision. and sometimes that fork in the road goes the right way, and sometimes it doesn't and goes to a Dead End.

I can never emphasize too much that those times of Pathos, Angst, Consternation and Lament in our lives are probably one of the greatest teachers we have in life. Yes - "teachers" - because when things go smoothly we don't work hard. When stuff just happens, and we keep rolling without strife, we don't have to work and figure things out because stuff just happens.

But when we go through frustrating and difficult times, during those moments of angst and pathos and lament is when we start to sort things out, and learn. When something goes awry, and we don't get a quick easy answer, we start to work it out and learn. And learn...

For instance, a simple example would be if you live in a neighborhood for years and years. Then somebody asks directions to a place you've gone to a hundred times. You try to tell them how to get there, but you are not sure of the name of the streets, and you say things like, "it's the third street, I think. Then go four blocks, and turn again, but I don't remember the name of the street, I drive it all the time, but I just know how to get there."

Or when you're working on your computer, and you do things in your Word Program, but trying to explain exactly to someone which button, key, or process you use, can be boggling because you've done it so many times, it is second nature to you. And you don't think about it as you do it.

Life gets that way too! It just happens, and we don't always appreciate it when we take it for granted. I also like the bumper sticker and use it many times to prod thinking: "Are we having FUN Yet?" A lot of times people don't know that they're having fun until they stop and think about it. They don't realize what they had until it's not there - and they've reached the point of lament over the loss of what they had. When you miss something is when you start to realize what it meant to you before. And it's when you start appreciating what ever it is that you're now missing.

For example, I always have had excellent vision, most of my life, my distance vision has been better than average, at 20/15. I've shared a lot of my life with many people who were very nearsighted. I could understand a bit of their frustration at not seeing well, but it still didn't mean as much to me as it does now that I am at the point where I have old guy eyes - i.e., having to have reading glasses on, and different ones for different things. UGH. I find myself now having to work at seeing and adjusting my eyes constantly, instead of just looking at something without making it into a damn project! I now appreciate how wonderful my eyesight was, now I can understand more my friends who were not able to read the clock across the room without their glasses, or one of my friends was so nearsighted, he always had to put his glasses on to go to the bathroom in the middle of the night, he wore his glasses in the shower, he would even wear his glasses swimming. I remember him wearing them up to the diving board walking to the end of the diving board to check it out then running back to hang his glasses on a little hook - then diving in and hoping he could find his glasses again when he got back out from diving. Damn, what a lot of work to enjoy something that to me was simple - dive into the pool. I now appreciate what struggles he went through and realize I took for granted looking at the clock in the morning, looking out the window whenever I wanted, being able to swim and not worry about where I was.

Take a few minutes to appreciate what you have and reflect on the Gifts that you do have, many that you take for granted until a Loss comes into your life. Almost every day that I am home, I go onto the roof patio of our condo, and look around at the millions of lights and people in LA, at the planes landing at the airport, at the stars twinkling in the sky and I am humbled and take time to appreciate the gifts I have.

You will not be the first to reflect on such things. There are many poems, songs, books and movies written about appreciating what we have, and not missing them during our Journey called Life.

Here is one of those songs I love, it's an old Mama Cass song from many years ago, listen to the words and reflect about the last time you did some of these things?

13

Did you ever lie and listen to a rainfall?
Did you ever eat a homemade apple pie/
Did you ever watch a child while he was praying?
Just don't let the good life pass you by.

Did you ever hold a hand to stop its trembling?
Did you ever watch the sun desert the sky?
Did you ever hold a mate while they're sleeping?
Friend, don't let the good life pass you by.

Man was made for loving not for lying,
Don't give him all the things he really needs,
Just look my friend, there is
HAPPINESS in living,
somewhere between broke and being free.

Did you ever see the sunny side of losing?
Did you ever sit right down and have a cry?
Did you ever take the time to help a neighbor?
Just don't let the good life pass you by.

And a last parting shot along this theme is this quote which comes from a '70's song.

This one also brings up lots of thoughts for us all to reflect on and a point I make later on about LOOKING and SEEING. There is a world around you to behold. And a world to learn from, it is what we learn after we know everything, that means so much...

"There is none so blind
as he who will not see,
We mustn't close our minds
but let our thoughts be free,
for every hour that's passing by,
the world is a little older,
Its time to realize that beauty lies
in the eyes of the beholder."

# PART ONE

# Pathos, Angst, Consternation and Lament

It's funny, but did you ever notice that it is during times of **Pathos, Angst, Consternation and Lament**, we normally do our most productive work. Seldom have great works such as plays, scripts, books, or those damn country western songs, ever been produced by 'happy folks, doing well, and kicking back, enjoying life'. Heck, even the BIBLE was written during times of grief, angst and strife!

I have certainly been productive in the last few years with the struggling economy, and loss of a number of friends to moving, end of relationships and death. I have been provided with plenty of Pathos, Angst, Consternation and Lament! Not since the loss of my partner 18 years ago, have I had such a stirring of emotions and feelings as I had recently. In this wake, there has been lots of productive projects, writing of books, and movement. And a year and a half ago when I almost died with a 105.1 F. temperature and laid for 10 days in a hospital with staff saying, "Damn, we almost lost you." And a car accident where someone lost control of their SUV and sideswiped me at 70 mph on a busy Maryland Parkway at rush hour where I got slammed into the center divider, and thanks to 1.5 million miles of driving experience, a great rental car, LOTS of luck, and God's grace, I ground to a halt with no front tires, riding on the car frame, a totaled car, but for me... just a small contusion on my head! It was the SECOND **NDE** (near death experience) for me in two years!! I wanted to cry recently when I was doing some of this writing, prompted by these things, but it was more for happiness, to be OK after that horrible close call with health in the hospital, and then the accident.

It is those moments, when we reflect on our pain, our losses, but then realize and appreciate humbly what we do have, that we can write, compose and create.

Think about it: it's in times of strife that we work the hardest and that we DON'T take things for granted. When a country is in a Recession, we have to THINK about what to spend money on, how to make money, and how to survive. When the economy is booming, we can spend freely, start any kind of silly business and not worry about retirement or anything. Now, however, we have to put some thought into what we are doing.

So - Pathos, Angst, Consternation and Lament - can be put to good use.

Don't panic. Understand, that if you have experienced a Loss and are: Feeling Depressed; sad all the time; wondering if you can get through this; feeling like you've run out of energy or out of time; thinking what to do - what to do? That's all normal.

First of all, it is a difficult time. It's not that you are going crazy, or that you can't control emotions. Things are tough. It's not your imagination. But YOU will make it, and we'll talk about things to help you get through it. I'm going to give you suggestions for NOW and ways to cope and some suggestions for what you can do with, and for, YOUR future. Things to help you with the long term, and the rest of your life. Together we can get

20

through this! Hang in there.

Now - today - it's time to move forward and manage your life through this difficult time. Can this feeling of Depression and Loss ever offer something positive? We'll talk about how Depression is a good thing in a bit.

First of all, Yes, there is lots of Clinical Depression when we experience loss, but it is appropriate and doesn't require a person to run to the Doctor for meds to control their fears, tears, or pain!! Just telling someone to 'get over it', or that 'time heals all wounds' won't do the trick either. And, remember, in your lifetime, you will experience more losses, but each time hopefully you will also GROW.

Part of my philosophy. when I talk about the end not really being The End, or that what we call the end is actually the beginning or start of something new, comes from my experiences in the mid to late '80s and early '90s of being one of the first counselors for the state of California hired by the state of California to do AIDS testing. In the early days, we had different names, HLTV3 and HIV counselor, but we were never called AIDS counselors. In reality, in 1985 when I started at the clinic with two other therapists, no doctors in LA County or the surrounding counties were doing AIDS tests of any sort. And only one hospital in the area, County General downtown, would even allow an AIDS patient to be in their hospital. So the scenario I dealt with in 1985 when I first started at the clinic was one where people would come in very sick, often basically on their deathbed. They usually had been sent in by their doctor to confirm that they did have AIDS which the doctors assumed was due to the presence of various Immune Diseases that only AIDS patients were getting.

A few years after we opened for testing, some AIDS clinics opened up, and some AIDS wings opened up in some of the area hospitals. But in those first two years particularly working at the clinic testing site, there were many times when the people were so sick that all we at the clinic could do was to pack them in a taxi, or call the paramedics, and ship them off to County General Hospital for their last ride.

It was rough to give results, and sit across the desk, with somebody 2 feet away from you, who might look at you with pleading eyes, hoping you were going to tell them they were okay but instead you were telling them bad news. It was very traumatic on trained therapists to be telling people basically a "final type news". Going into the field of therapy, we had always planned on working with patients where we would be telling them there was hope - the reason for coming for therapy is to make things better. Here we were having to tell people that things were over. Final news. One newspaper that interviewed us as the 3 founding AIDS counselors for the State, showed the 3 of us standing in the clinic with smiles, and the title of the article read "GRIM REAPERS deliver the bad news!"

As I've mentioned elsewhere in the book, I told 3500 people or so that they were HIV positive, and basically confirming an AIDS diagnosis, which in the 1980's was most often a death sentence. One Saturday I remember some young men who had been part of my youth group at my church in Ventura County who came in to test. There were four guys, they were now all students at a local college. Two of them had been in the youth group, and the other two were friends of theirs from college. They wanted me personally to give the test results because they knew me. And they felt safer doing that. All four were positive with HIV. All four, at the time were very healthy that day. However, one young man, Tony, developed full-blown AIDS within about eight months of his test results. He was dead within a year at the age of 22. Another of the young men developed the disease somewhat later in life and expired. The other two are long-term survivors. One of those two has had an ongoing battle with the virus and the other one is one of those folks that science is examining trying to find out how come there are some people where the virus does not seem to affect them.

I remember sitting with a 77-year-old gentleman who had been with his male partner for 55 years. They had met when they were each 22 years old. They had a wonderful long term relationship and had been monogamous. However, the gentleman had received a letter in the mail from Cedars Hospital that a transfusion he had received in recent years for some surgery had been tested and shown to be positive with HIV. This 77 year old taught me a lot that day, quickly. I felt bad having to tell him that what he was experiencing probably was AIDS-related, and that his time left might be short. But, he was one of those wonderful ones who handled it with such dignity and grace that most of his energy went into reassuring me, as the counselor, that I had done a good job in delivering the news in a way that showed respect for him, for his life and life in general. A very nice gentleman. He reminded me he had lived a good long time. That he had had a wonderful long-term relationship, and that it was 'okay'. He was handling it better than I was! He certainly handled the bad news with "dignity and grace." Amazing.

There were many cases where either I might have already known the people for various reasons, whether they were just people I had seen on the streets of our area, or were well-known people from the media, or people that I just got to know very intensely in those few minutes of giving results. We were allowed 45 minutes to an hour for positive results, i.e., telling somebody that they were likely infected with the AIDS virus. We were allowed 15 minutes of our schedule for negatives. It was odd when I would train counselors for other parts of the country and the world, to do test results, and they would sit in with us to do results. I would explain to them what they had learned about short term "Brief Therapy" was going out the window! Many, who had been therapists for many years would say, "Oh, I understand about brief therapy, I often work with clients for only two or three months to help them through a trauma." At that point I would remind them that as AIDS counselors, delivering the hard news, we didn't have the luxury of two or three months, but that we were probably going to have to deal with **D.A.B.D.A.** - DENIAL, ANGER, BARGAINING, DEPRESSION, ACCEPTANCE- i.e., going from Denial to Acceptance in 45 minutes or less!

This meant that we opened up the wound in their lives, presented a trauma for them, but we as therapists didn't get to follow through and get closure. In most cases for a therapist, the client comes to you with a problem - it may be depression or it might be separation and eventual divorce. But, as a therapist you get to work

24

with them for a period of time, normally months. And you get to see them through their progress, through the difficult period. You get to see the results. If it goes well you can take credit for your success. If it doesn't go well, you can always use the excuse, that they were such a mess when they came in that you couldn't do anything for them! But you would have some closure, either positive or negative. For us early AIDS counselors, telling thousands of people they were possibly going to die and for many in the early days, likely going to die much sooner than later, it didn't allow closure for the therapists/counselors. One small amount of closure provided for us was that the county hospital AIDS unit nurses would actually call us and inform us if somebody we had sent down either in the cab or the ambulance or referred directly down, had died. It would give us a moment of closure, with sadness, but closure.

I, for one, would watch the obituary columns, particularly those that had pictures because our clinic was anonymous and we didn't have names of the people we were giving results to - just their zip codes, and their ages. Seeing an obit with a face I recognized gave me pause to reflect, and a moment to grieve.

It was rough for us as therapists. Of the three of us at that clinic we all had some kind of an epiphany where and when, we realized how much being the 'grim reapers' it had impacted us. One of the counselors went home one afternoon after delivering quite a few positive test results, and her partner reported later that she found her sitting in the bathtub crying. She had come home from the clinic - they had a large home with lots of clothes and lots of closets - and the counselor had apparently run from closet to closet to closet and organized everything by colors and sizes and even hanger colors! And finally, exhausted from putting the closets in order (something she couldn't do for the people she was working with), she settled into the tub in tears. Realizing that even if she put all the black plastic hangers in one closet and the white plastic hangers in another closet, and all the yellow shirts in one closet in order next to the red shirts or what ever, even with that much order in her life she could still not control the results she was giving to our clients. It was a psychological way for her to attempt to put some "order" in the chaos that was now present in her life. She knew that one day she might go to the clinic and give out many test results that told people they were fine, and feel very good. But then there were those other days, when she felt that she had disrupted and sometimes destroyed someone's hope and life.

The other counselor came in one day and said that he had this dream that he and his partner had gone on a cruise ship. In his dream, he got mad at his partner because they were sitting on the deck sunning in chaise lounges when the ship started to rock violently in the waves. Slowly the fully occupied chaise lounges started to roll towards the edge of the ship and go over the side. There were hundreds of chaise lounges with folks on the deck, and he realized most of the people were sick. He got mad at his partner because, remember, again this is in a dream, he yelled at his partner to help him try to keep these people from going over the side. His partner just stood there lost, and said, "Sorry, I don't know what to do." When this counselor and I talked about that dream, we realized his frustration wasn't just trying to save the people, but he was feeling that nobody cared, and nobody else was trying to help him. That what he was doing on board the ship was futile, and this transferred over to his role at the clinic, and how he felt many times when he could offer no help to saving the lives of the people he was dealing with. And that the person who he lived with did not understand his sorrow.

The point here is for you to realize that even so-called trained professionals, licensed professionals with years of experience and lots of college courses about this stuff, also have problems in dealing with Loss. In the early days of AIDS, we had special support groups for AIDS care workers. We would sit around and talk about ways that we coped with dealing with something that could be as depressing as having to tell people they're going to die. It was funny, one counselor reported that she liked to crochet Afghans, and that she had made so many Afghans that she didn't know what she was going to do with them. But she realized that after a day of disrupting lives, then realizing she couldn't help some of the people make things "better" that she could do something that showed positive results - and that was to make Afghans, tangible positive results.

Between being an AIDS counselor, and early Hospice counselor dealing with cancer patients, plus my last stint, being on staff at the stroke rehab unit, I have watched a lot of my clients and patients die, yes, die - not pass on, not go to their final resting place, not just go to sleep, but - die. And somebody said to me don't you feel that every time you lose somebody part of you dies with them. Well, we've all lost somebody or been around people who have had somebody close to them die, and amidst their tears, we hear them say that part of them died when this person died. Elsewhere in this book there's a poem from a mother who found her teenage son had committed suicide. In it she refers to having found her son at 9 AM in the morning hanging in his bedroom. She mentions that the coroner declared that he had probably died eight hours before, at about 1 AM. She states eloquently that her son "died at 1 AM, and I died that morning at 9 AM."

I'm a chubby guy, and the only reason why I share that with you is that if a little bit of me died or went with everybody who I've dealt with when they died, I'd be very thin and slim! The truth is that what I have learned and what I try to share with you, is that while part of me has died with those who preceded me, from those same folks that I was the closest to or had a special relationship with, or special friendship with, I have taken something forward from them. In other words they have left something special with me and they've added to my life and made my life fuller.

For instance I remember talking with one of my patients at the hospital who was in his 80s. His wife Lila, was lying in the bed and running out of time. Her hubby Fred was sitting next to the bed asking me, "Is my little girl gonna be okay?" I had to tell him, "No, Fred she's on her way." And as we sat and talked he mentioned they'd been together over 30 years. Having good math skills, I realized that 30 minus 80 equals 50. So yes he confirmed he had married her when he was 52 after his first wife, and after Lila's first husband, had died. I gently questioned him about his love for Lila and his love for his first wife, Barbara. He explained that he'd dearly loved

Barbara too, and he knew that she loved him. And he explained, that when he met Lila, his love for Lila did not negate his love for Barbara. Instead, he said, "Remember, part of my success in my relationship with Lila can be attributed to the wonderful relationship I had with my first love, Barbara, and learning from her how to love and be loved. And her helping to teach me how to love and be loved." Thirdly, he reminded me that his time with Barbara was at a different place at a different time in his life. And he acknowledged that maybe if he had met Lila back then, they might never have gotten married or worked things out. But the timing was right the way it was. Right time, right place.

Remember, we really can gain, and learn from those who die, and honor their presence in our lives by making differences in our lives as we go forward. Thus while we give away a little of us each time somebody dies, we also keep part of them with us, and inside of us, as we go forward live richer lives because of our time with them. As part of my prayer routine, I thank the people who have contributed to my life in the past, and thank them for what they have given or inspired in me, so that I can go on living today and make things better for other people.

## THE NOW PART - ATTITUDE

Remember, the only thing you can arm yourself with most days is - the **right attitude**. Attitude or faith means a lot in all situations.

Way back in 1932, Charles Swindoll said:

"The longer I live, the more I realize the impact of attitude on life. I believe the single most significant decision I can make on a day-to-day basis is my choice of attitude. Attitude, to me, is more important than facts. It is more important than the past, my education, my bankroll, my successes or failures, fame or pain, what other people think of me or say about me, my circumstances, or my position. It will make or break a company, a friendship, a relationship or a home. The remarkable thing is we have a choice everyday regarding the attitude we will embrace for that day. We cannot change our past... we cannot change the fact that people will act in a certain way. We cannot change the inevitable. The only thing we can do is play on the one asset we have, and that is our attitude. I am convinced that life is 10% what happens to me and 90% of how I react to it."

And so it is with you too... You are in charge of your Attitude. Attitude keeps us going on or cripples our progress. Attitude alone fuels our fire or assaults our hope. When our attitudes are right, no valley too deep, no dream too extreme, no challenge too great for us no matter how difficult your loss is at the time.

In keeping with our theme about attitude, one of the things we have to do is deal with reality and our egos. I'm going to toss in here something that is rather sobering, but it is reality. A number of years ago a dear friend of mine and colleague, David Taylor, shared with me something he learned when he would go on his yearly religious retreat. Originally, David had planned on going into the priesthood but got derailed when he ended up in a lifelong relationship but he still had strong religious beliefs and enjoyed yearly going to a week long retreat at a seminary in the Malibu Mountains. It was his time for reflection and personal growth. The emphasis was on silence and to be with your inner thoughts and make peace for yourself, and with yourself. He shared a mantra that they repeated every morning before breakfast, then after breakfast until the next morning at breakfast they were to stay silent. Breakfast was a time for discussion and sharing.

This is a paraphrase of the much more involved mantra that they repeated every day. Its purpose is to get to the point of reality and clarity, and get out of the way some of the garbage that we impact our lives with. There are some realities that we fret over that are just that: fretting. And no matter how much we fret, the world will not benefit from our fretting! For instance, unless there is a major celestial trauma, the sun will come up tomorrow, night time will come, some people will be selfish, some people will be kind. The gist of the mantra about life that was repeated every day is:

You will get old.
You will get sick.
And... You will... die.
Your friends will get old,
they will get sick,
and... they will die.
**Now - Get on with living!**

When you reflect on this mantra, think about how much energy we all spend in fighting a flu or cold instead of realizing that sometimes the body needs rest and one of the ways of getting that rest is becoming sick. We feel like we're a failure when we get a cold. Everyone has been around someone at work who shows up miserable, with a runny nose, and a sore throat and proudly announces as they are coughing and hacking, "I'm not going to let this cold get me." Well maybe the cold isn't getting them but it's going to get you and everybody around them. They should stay home and let their body heal.

You will get old. Get over it! My god, how much money is spent coloring our hair, doing Botox, plastic surgery to get rid of wrinkles, money spent on weird clothes or impractical cars that are going to make us look young and feel young. Women particularly, can get very angry if their true ages are identified. I believe strongly that we should look in the mirror, look at those wrinkles, look at the gray hairs, and mostly be proud of ourselves that we've made it this far, and hopefully proud of ourselves for what we've accomplished to this date. I have a T-shirt that says, "I'm not Aging, I'm Fermenting." The mentality being that with  time, I'm getting better - like a good wine.

Many years ago a young friend of mine asked me if I would like to live over again. At that point I was in my 50's. I hesitated, and he interjected immediately - "Well, okay, what if you could know what you know now, but could live over?" Needless to say, most of us feel that we wouldn't want to give up the knowledge that we have now to start Life over.

But my friend was surprised when I turned around

instead and said, "Josh, I think that when my run of Life is over, and I reach the end of that journey, I should probably just leave with some dignity and grace." There is always a right time to exit. And for old folks particularly, it's important to work on our legacy so that when we do leave this Earth we have left something special. Yep, its all about Attitude. Attitude.

## GRIEF

I presented the following lecture on GRIEF & the Feeling of Loss when I was training AIDS counselors to deal with the Grief they might experience in constantly delivering the heavy news. Years later, I presented it for my staff at the stroke unit where they also had to deal with THEIR feelings, as they realized many of their patients might not survive, and most would not go home perky and fine, but in a diminished state of health. HOWEVER many of those patients also exhibited an extraordinarily positive attitude that gave some staff the needed drive to keep rollin.

Ironically, Baby Boomers and Seniors can relate to many of these thoughts too, because as we age and our address books diminish in size as our friends age and die, and our calendars are harder to fill with folks who are able to 'get around' or drive, or even feel like leaving home!

## "Grief and the Feeling of Loss"

"Grief is what happens in your mind and body when someone close to you dies. Your pain is deep, and your emotions may seem to be overwhelming. It involves expressing some of your deepest and most intimate feelings. Gradually you will begin to notice that there are times when the hurt is not so great. This will be a sign that healing is taking place.

"The AIDS CRISIS brings us monthly, weekly, and sometimes daily, in touch with losses. As life partners, close friends, and even people we see daily at the store or supermarket, are diagnosed, or who die, our losses don't fade. One passes, and another gets sick in front of your eyes. The natural healing process is impeded, and our loss grows into anger. We realize more and more that we are mortal, we feel impotent - unable to bring back the dead, and unable to stop many of your friends from dying. We feel helpless, angry, guilty, alone. We need to cry, and... to talk and vent. It takes great courage to risk feeling the depths of loss. Being left by someone close to you is a form of abandonment. Loneliness and isolation is the worst problem for people whose spouses and life partners have died.

"The passage of time helps to ease the pain of grief; however, in the current AIDS situation, we are constantly exposed to additional losses and need to be aware of our need for support. Support groups are a good place to vent the feeling, share with others who have similar loss feelings, where you can vocalize your feelings.

"The hurt does not disappear entirely, but the intensity of the pain lessens with time. In a way, as we say good bye to our friends, whether it be in silence, or at a memorial service letting balloons into the air, or a poem we write in our own personal journals, death experiences can bring new strength and open the way to new growth.

"It has been suggested recently in a talk by Los Angeles Psychotherapist, J. Gelfand, that there are similarities in the present situation of AIDS "survivors" and with Holocaust survivors. The overwhelming feelings of a community hit most hard by the disease - the gay community - experiences the burden of woe. This feeling is similar to the frightening situation of the Jews seeing their friends and family get detached from them and killed, while helplessly watching them die. There was the stigma of being Jewish that stood on their minds, as the "stigma" of being gay, and with many folks assuming that it was somewhat deserved for being gay... and that gays are expendable.

Dr. G."

NOTE: The following page is a very moving, and provoking blog that exemplifies grief in a way that no textbook description could even begin to show. Entered here exactly as it was written in her own words, and writing style - grammar and all.

# Why?
### By Timmy's Mom

4-13-01 was a beautiful Saturday morning in Georgia. I had gotten up to get my coffee, saw Tim's light was on and thought wow he's up early for a Sat morn. I was getting ready to go walking when the phone rang. It was Sam, Tim's girlfriend. "Hang on", I said, "I'll go get him."

We were fixing Tim's room in our garage about 50ft from our house. He didn't really have a room of his own in the house, our house is so small. We had gotten his cable turned on just 2 weeks before. He had only slept there a couple nights, it had been too cold. He had stars everywhere on the ceiling, he and his friends loved sleeping under the stars in his room.

I went to his door but the sofa was pushed up against it. I could only see the frayed end of a rope. Went to the side door to find a dummy hanging next to the front door, the rope was Tim's hair. Thinking how much trouble he was in for hanging a dummy, he knew better! Wondering where he was and thinking that maybe the boys had came by early to pick him up. I knew they were playing that day. Noticed that the Dummy has on Tim's clothes. I stepped a little closer to see fluid running from my baby's nose. We think and I'm almost sure he broke his neck. Running back to the phone to tell Sam that Tim had hanged himself and I had to call 911. Alan came to the door telling me, it's Tim and he's already cold.

That is the Minute I Died!

Tim died on 4-13-01 between 10 and 11pm. I died 4-14-01 at 9:15am.

WHY GOD - I don't understand, could it of been your will for my son to die? Could this of been for my sake, that I might be a better person or draw closer to thee Lord?

How could you allow my son to die such a horrible death?

Am I suppose to learn from this? Am I such a bad person that my whole world had to be taken?

Am I supposed to give thanks for this pain, for the lessons I've learned or the person I've become? Is this grief supposed to make me stronger in some way? I don't understand God, how am I suppose to live from day to day?

Am I, Lord supposed to feel your arms around me? How can I have the strength to carry on?

Am I supposed to be strong in my way of thinking? Are you telling me Lord that I need to help others?

Perhaps I am just suffering and stubborn. Do I, Lord need to have more faith, open my arms and trust in thee?

16 years, 16 years of living, of Heaven, of school projects, of waiting for the bus, of baby sitter's, of raising the most wonderful little boy on earth.

16 years of you sleeping with me every Christmas Eve night, of fairies and money under your pillow. Of dental trips and hair cuts, of reading your picture Bible and teaching.

16 years of thanking God each day for this wonderful blessing. Of blonde hair blue eyes and watching Tim grow.

Of being there when you were happy, scared or in trouble.

Of notes from your teachers. Of having my heart torn out each time a girl broke yours.

Of watching you being a silent mime.

16 years of picking out your clothes, of hearing you call

for "mama".

16 years of hide and seek and watching you bounce from cushion to wall and back.

16 years of driving lessons, of hunting all over town for a job.

16 years of trying so hard to make you happy cuz you were all we had and I loved you so much.

... Of not knowing of your depression.

16 years of loving you!

----→⋈⋈←----

## "BUT, I'VE STILL GOT CHECKS?"

"But I've still got checks in my checkbook, how can I be broke?" With an incredulous look, and a lot of naivete, and after a few bounced checks, one can say with wonderment, "How can I be broke when there are still lots of checks in my checkbook?"

A few years ago, I visited my friend Shirley in Phoenix. Shirley is mid-80's. She has lived a good life. She feels fine, she is active, she has lots of friends and has done a lot of good things in her life, touched a lot of people. The doc tells her she has an aneurism near the brain, 70% clogged arteries, and a few other things. He also tells her that operating could kill her, and to just hang around til the aneurism blows, and she expires quietly. He said there wouldn't be much pain, just over in seconds. Her response, "How can I be so sick and not feel sick?"

Her life is like the checks in the checkbook - she's is cookin' along, she is having fun, she's running around in her golf cart, playing bingo, smiling and taking care of the 'old' folks in her mobile home park, but... her 'bank account of life' has run out and she's gonna be saying goodbye. Goin' out with a smile, and... leaving a few tears behind.

As I drove the 400 miles home, I listened to my friend Rod McKuen's music. I choked up and cried a bit, thought about lots. My life, Shirley's, and my friend Jane's too. It's spring, its Easter, it's the start of a new year, flowers blooming, summer is coming, things are good, but... I went to visit Shirley to say good bye, it's the autumn of her life. And right now, my friend Jane is slowly saying goodbye to her father too, the person who is her best and most trusted friend as well as her dad. His journey here is done, too.

Rod's song "Season's of the Sun" broadsided me as I drove, listened, and sang along with the music. Poignant and right on target with Shirley, and Jane... and for me - as I am about to hit the autumn of my life. Its hard to say Goodbye when Shirley still has LOTS of checks in her checkbook, lots of stories to tell, lots of kindness to share, and plenty more brownies to make for her family and friends... but her account has run out on this earth as we know it. And Jane knows its time for dad to leave, they have gone through all the seasons together, lived life fully, shared, talked and loved each other... but its still hard to say goodbye as the flowers bloom and the birds are singing.

Here are some lyrics from Rod's song...

"Adieu my friend, it's hard to die, when all the birds are singing in the sky. Now that the spring is in the air....

We had joy, we had fun we had seasons in the sun, but the hills that we climbed were just seasons out of time.

Adieu my friend, please pray for me, I was the black sheep of the family.

You tried to teach me right from wrong, Too much wine and too much song,

Wondered how I got along, Adieu my friend,  it's hard to die, when all the birds are singing in the sky.

Now that the spring is in the air, little children everywhere,

When you see 'em I'll be there."

Well, Shirley, we had joy, we had fun, we had seasons in the Arizona sun, but the wine and the song, like the seasons have all gone. You'll have left your legacy, now Goodbye, Shirley, my friend, it's hard for you to die when all the birds are singing in the sky, now that the spring is in the air. With the flowers everywhere. I wish that we could both be there.

# PART TWO

## OUR REACTIONS TO LOSS

There is a wide spectrum of emotions, thoughts and reactions we experience when there is a sudden or expected loss in our lives. Remember, not everyone follows the same pattern, there is NO test given, or points awarded for grieving 'right'. We do know from past experience and observations, that there are some patterns that exist in a majority of people who grieve over losses. There are hundreds of shades of gray, nuance and exceptions. No one is exactly like another; we are shaped by our biology, family and community environment, religious background, cultural norms and individual personality.

### The Obvious

We are told by our parents, families, friends, lovers, religions, cultures, society and the media how to react. Most folks can grieve the same way, though as noted further on, in most cultures, men are expected to grieve in a slightly different way and the idea of 'remaining strong' in our culture in the United States at least, means to really impede the grieving process for them, and stay stuck rather than process out their grief.

How we grieve is complex and what folks need to do to process out their grief is often impeded because family and friends want the person to move on from their loss ASAP (as soon as possible). These are often the people around you, your support system, but they want to see healing ASAP, and don't want you to suffer - and for some it's a bit selfish too, because they want their old

43

happy person back - now. Some of these messages are blatant and others more subtle. Some are non-verbal and observed by actions and deeds.

An example of this occurred for me after the death of my partner, one day as I was walking down the hallway of our condo building, the lady who cleans the building saw me smile. In the first month, there had been very little smiling, and as soon as she saw the smile, she immediately commented "Oh, I am so glad you are doing well and moving on. I'm glad you're getting over it." No, I really was not "over it" but the constant sadness was fading slightly, allowing a smile here and there. What I realized was that she didn't like to deal with grieving or sadness and did not want to see people around her in that spot. Her happiness over my smile, had little to do with me. But more to do with her not having to deal with my being sad. While I was on staff at the hospital and the stroke rehab unit, and in dealing with illness and my partner, I made the observation that many people seem to be afraid to come visit folks in the hospital, and were particularly concerned about coming to see people who might be what we would consider terminal. I think in their minds, there was the concern that they would be "catching death".

So people often are not thinking of your feelings, but they are having to deal with their own fears that they don't know how to handle your sadness, or it can be bringing up their own issues that they haven't handled in themselves. Many times over the years and working with hospitals, I have had to restrict visitors for patients.

Those who are quite ill whether it's because they just went through surgery or just recently had a stroke, or those who were terminal, would get very drained when people would come to visit them. Particularly if they had been a happy friendly person like my friend Martha for instance. Martha ended up dying of cancer back in the 1970's. She was on staff at the school where I was teaching, she was sort of what I guess we might call 'the spark plug' of the staff. She was always smiling, she only had nice things to say about people, and she always had a word or two of support that would make you feel good. When Martha was getting towards the end, I could see how rough it was for her as people would arrive, theoretically, to make her feel better and visit with her. However, in reality, when they would walk in and see this formerly perky, wonderful lady, who now was very frail, thin and not looking well, she would sense their shock. In turn, she would have to work at making them feel better before they left. She would joke about being out to play tennis again with them at some point, or having dinner again soon, but she wasn't going to be. But it became her duty to make people feel better when they came to see her. It took too much energy from her that was needed to keep her rolling along the lines. So I wrote the recommendation that restricted her visits to the people who can handle it and who SHE doesn't have to make feel better and take away HER energy!

When someone loses a loved one, by death or separation, they can be thrown into an unknown world of pain that casts their beliefs, personal expectations and accepted ways of being into an ocean of doubt, turmoil and isolation. Loss can cause an eruption of feelings, fears and thoughts that fly in the face of what it has

45

meant to normal, and we think we are going crazy. In a way, there is logic to grieving and in many ways, it is illogical. Each one grieves in a different way, at a different pace, yet there still tends to be a pattern. But no one is graded in how they grieve! Or graded down for not doing it well!!

It's not unusual when someone loses someone close to them and the pain starts to hit, for them to immediately ask, "Tell me what to do. How do I fix this? There must be some steps or some way to move on." Such efforts at avoiding, "toughing it out" or "getting rid" of the pain of loss usually result in temporary relief and rarely change the reality of the condition. The pain of grief is one of the few kinds of pain in life that are best dealt with head on, by doing something men are often taught to avoid. The pain of grief and mourning tend to change and heal with time and attention (not just time) when we can honestly acknowledge what we are feeling, thinking and believing and externalize such reactions in a positive, healthy environment and/or manner.

Women and children are better about verbalizing feelings and experiences. And, as part of the grieving, instead of crying and showing feelings, men often talk about safe things: the things they did for their loved one; how they took care of them; what they are doing now from dealing with insurance to arranging memorials to show they are still in control; what they plan to do in the future.

Anger, guilt and reasoning are ways we try to control and make sense out of our grief and the situation it has put us in. It doesn't actually give us any more control, but rather just a sense of control, of getting control back in our life.

## Intimacy

Remember at the time of loss of someone who was very close, such as spouse, sibling, parent or best friend, adding to that loss and intensity of the loss is the fact that the person who you would likely talk to at a time like this, IS the person who you have just lost.

I.e., if the person lost their spouse or partner, the person they normally would come home to, cry with, and share their feelings with, is the person who has just died! And in loss situations, this also applies to divorces, separations and ends of relationships. These are usually the people you feel the safest to share your innermost feelings with, and now they are no longer part of your life.

These are also the people you would turn to and need for intimate human contact as well as the emotional support. This normally is the person you might come home and curl up with, and now you miss them doubly.

When we lose a close person, it can be hard sometimes to hug, or embrace another.

There are no steadfast rules about when it is time to get involved with another person if it was a partner, spouse, or lover who died, or who left in separation or divorce but here are some of the options:

- Some may choose to never get married or in a relationship again and that's OK.
- Some will never forget the person lost, no matter if they join up with others in the future, nor how deeply in love and involved that new relationship becomes.
- Some times people want to get the person to "go out" again, not because they necessarily should or shouldn't, but because they want them to be

happy and they think another relationship will provide that kind of happiness and is the magic pill to "make you feel better" or "help you get over it".

- Most people who have experienced a good marriage or partnership have a natural desire, at some point in their lives, to repeat that experience.

People have to look closely and honestly at their motivation for companionship. How much of their wish to be with someone else is out of loneliness and need? What values or interests are they ignoring in order to "be with" someone else? Can the person they develop a new relationship with accept and understand that your deceased mate will always be part of your life?

Loving another person and being loved by another is a natural human need and desire. To do so shows no disrespect for the one who has died. There is plenty of room in our hearts to hold in it  the loved one who died, and love another. We don't have to throw one person out in order to make room for someone else.

Folks need to realize they will never have an identical love or relationship with another that they had with the person who died or left, but that doesn't mean they can't experience the same intensity or depth of connection with another. It will not be the same, but it can be just as profound and intimate.

While some people choose not to have another love in their life and are perfectly happy, others stay alone out of fear of another loss. I experience this also dealing with divorce situations, there is often a resistance to 'let their guard down' and get involved again, to be

HURT again in their minds. When we have lost a loved one to death or separation we are more aware than most of the reality of our limited lives and realize the fact that at some point in all relationships, either by one person choosing to leave or by death, one of us will leave the other. We consciously and most often unconsciously tell ourselves, "If I let myself love again and become intimate and attached to another, that person may leave me or die. I don't want to experience that kind of pain again."

These reactions and thoughts are entirely understandable. We all try to protect ourselves to varying degrees and lengths from painful experiences; but to do so at all costs ends up being too costly. It cuts us off from other aspects of life. The eternal Shakespearean question remains. "Is it better to have loved and lost, than never to have loved at all?" We must each find within ourselves when, how and/or if we choose to love again.

### Don't Just Sit There, Do Something!

When it comes to grief, loss and separation, mourning the loss of someone you love, adore, respect, hate, despise or have any combination of feelings toward takes time, attention and action. Sometimes grief can cause such exhaustion and lethargy that it can seem impossible to do anything other than get through the day. The irony is that once you get moving, emoting or acting it usually increases your motivation, energy and health.

Once we have taken the time to acknowledge our loss (whatever it may be) and understand the impact and changes it is causing in our lives, we can then find ways to relieve, release, expel, create, explore and/or honor those feelings, sensations, thoughts, memories and beliefs.

Grief can involve the most painful emotions we have ever experienced. It is natural and understandable to want them to stop. One would have to be a masochist if they wanted such feelings to remain. Thus we ask ourselves, and God, the understandable question, "When will it stop? We pray it to end."

Unlike most kinds of pain where medical attention or medication can remedy the situation, the pains of grief are hard to shake, avoid or medicate. If it was advantageous to avoid or medicate ourselves after a death, we would encourage people to do so; but usually such avoidance or use of chemicals to numb the body, heart and mind's reactions to separation simply delays, suppresses or complicates matters.

Though there are thousands of ways to positively release the pressure cooker of emotion and suffering that death and separation can cause, here are a few brief suggestions -

Attend and/or create a service or event for the person who has died - these services are actually for those still living and gives them a safe place to vent and emote. Gatherings for the dead have many names - funerals, memorials, remembrances, wakes, celebrations and send-offs. They may be different in form, intent, content and cultural expectation, but they all speak to our human need to acknowledge the profound experience of death and make some sense out of loss. Whether public or private, families, relatives and friends gathering to proclaim the life and death of someone they knew is a centuries old ritual that can provide comfort, solace and support.

Funerals give us the opportunity to say, "Yes, my loved one has died. Yes, other people recognize the fact of their death. I am not alone in this experience. In the midst of death, among the living is the memory of the one who died. Yes, I see that their life has had an impact on others as well as me. Their life was significant. Their existence in my life had and will continue to have meaning."

Eat properly and take care of your self, try to eat one good meal a day and then one 'comfort food' if that makes you feel better! But get that one GOOD one in for sure. Vitamins help too.

Exercise; even when you don't feel like it. Walk, run, swim, hike, bicycle, workout, dance at least two to three times a week by yourself or with others. Be physical!

Rest and drink lots of water to counteract our body's dehydration during grief and sorrow.

Breathe deeply. Consciously take deep breaths throughout the day and evening. Listening to Meditation can be perfect for this. I have one that even starts with, "Now get comfortable, and Breathe-in deeply, now slowly release..." etc. You focus on your breathing, and for a few moments, that is your focus and not your loss and pain. It gives the body a few minutes to rebuild and heal so you can mourn more later. Breathing exercises, visualizations, relaxation, stretching, meditation, affirmations and yoga have all been scientifically shown to relieve stress, anxiety and provide positive endorphins to help the body heal.

Scream, wail, moan, sob, laugh hysterically, play music, sing, howl or cry out loud in the shower, on the floor, into a pillow, at the beach, in the woods.

Relax in a hot tub, hot bath, shower, sauna, sweat lodge or with a massage and let the emotion seep from your pores and evaporate with the steam.

Put together a collage, an altar, memory book, picture frame, treasure box, video about the person who died or left. Collect their memories in a safe spot where you can focus on them. Light a candle at the church.

Create a memorial, plant a tree, make a donation, volunteer, start an organization or dedicate an event, an action or your life to the loved one who has died. Some have created organizations or made a point of helping a neighbor, relative or buddy in honor of the person who died.

Write, talk, pray, light a candle, burn incense, look at a photo and/or have a conversation with, to or about the person who has passed away. Many people find that talking to the deceased helps soften the effects of their physical absence and supports them in maintaining an ongoing (though different) relationship and connection with the person who has died. Even if it is only for five to ten minutes, take a moment every day in some special place - your favorite corner of a room, in your garden, by the beach, in the redwoods, in a special park, at the grave side or with another person.

There is no right or wrong way to do it. How we live with the dead can also reflect and/or mirror how we choose to stay connected to and relate with those who are living.

After a death particularly, the person who is lost often shows up in our dreams. Rather than getting disturbed about it, I tell people to invite those "visits" and to even look forward to them. However our mind works, those visits can be very effective in healing as we share that time with the person.

I also recommend always, when dealing with loss from death, that the people become proactive rather than reactive in dealing with the mourning.

For instance, on that person's birthday or on the anniversary date of their passing, it's good to take the day off if you can from work, or plan ahead to have dinner with a friend who understands, and you can raise a toast to the person you lost. For myself, sometimes I take advantage of those days, and go for a long ride with music that I enjoyed with the person, and drive and talk out loud to them, and allow the tears to come as needed. That way I have some control over the crying and emotion, and it doesn't blind side me in the middle of an important meeting, or a class lecture, and it gives me the chance to allow the full emotion out without having to hide any of it.

Keep going. Don't give up. There IS a light at the end of the tunnel, even when you're in the depths of darkness. Life changes, feelings change, attitudes change, perceptions change and our understanding and appreciation of life are often awakened in the painful process of mourning.

Don't let anyone tell you exactly what you should do, or any list stop you from finding your own way to act, walk, crawl, run, jump or dance on your unique, individual journey of living as a man or woman with the reality of loss. You don't have to ignore or try to "get over" grief and mourning by avoiding or suppressing it. Use it as a catalyst, as fertilizer, as an open door inviting change, growth and transformation. Don't just sit there, yes - do something!

Men's reactions are all the same and yet at times different. There are an abundance of cliches about the differences between men and women and how they react to grief and sadness. Yes, there are differences: biological (different brains) & environmental (learned behavior) that affect how they perceive and react to loss.

There is a wide spectrum of emotions, thoughts and reactions which men experience when there is a sudden or expected loss in their life. The following does not apply to all men all the time, but are observations about some patterns that exist within a majority of men in grief. There are hundreds of shades of gray, nuances and exceptions. No man is exactly like another; they are shaped by Nature/heredity and individual personality, and Nurture/family, community, religion, culture. Men are not from Mars and Women are not from Venus. Men AND women are all born and die on the same planet - Earth.

## Men and Grief

Men are told by their parents, families, friends, lovers, religions, governments and the media to stay in control, be strong, grin and bear it, be providers, endure to the bitter end, win at all costs, act logically, perform, achieve, don't cry and above all - be in control. Some of these messages are blatant and others more subtle. Some are proclaimed orally or in print and others are non-verbal and observed by actions and deeds. They all tell boys that in order to be a "real man" you must never ever express or convey fear, dependence, loneliness, weakness, passivity or insecurity. When men are hurt growing up, they are told to "get up and shake it off". That is one reason it can feel so overwhelming when a man experiences the natural reactions to loss and grief and they can't just "shake it off" and carry on as if nothing has happened.

When men lose a loved one whether it be due to death, or other separation, they are thrown into an unknown world. Men tend to think in a linear fashion and want simple direct answers - or at least they think they do! If something disrupts their life, if someone dies, or leaves them, it can throw them for a loop if there is no clear cut map or 'service manual' to fix the problem or get back on the road.

Efforts are taken to avoid the pain which usually results in temporary relief - alcohol, working out, anger - that rarely changes the reality of the condition, instead of dealing with the pain and grief directly.

Men will often get mad at the doctor or nurses, when dealing with terminal illnesses or a traumatic death of loved one and blame them for the death. They will be angry the doctor didn't save them, and blame the docs and often then feel some guilt themselves for not having chosen the right doctor, or being mad that they themselves couldn't have done something to save or help them.

Men tend to speak "about" instead of "with" feelings. They don't like talking about how they feel, or being asked how they feel. They assume they should have a handle on their 'feelings' and that feelings should have absolutely NO control over them. They can talk about their "reactions" to something, or they can tell you a story "about" the deceased or separated person and get to the feelings, but then be a bit embarrassed if they start to show those feelings. As they tell you the story, they can tell you they HAVE painful feelings and reactions, but again, they are afraid to show them. REAL MEN don't cry! Often when a close person or relative dies, it brings up a lifetime of conflicted emotions.

They can tell you their reactions after a death, but then often you find they are busying themselves in work or in taking care of the rest of the family, so they don't have to 'feel' the feelings. When the journey through grief is presented as a so-called logical, problem-solving cognitive activity that men can get a handle on, and feel they can do something to control it, they are much more likely to connect and allow themselves to process and identify with what they are experiencing.

They want to know a way to get past this. Emphasizing, get PAST it. Not process it. Men do better at 'feeling' stuff if they are active, and when they do things like going for a walk, especially if it is something they did with the deceased, or taking the dog for a walk, feeling safe that the dog can share the feelings and NOT be judgmental of them. Sometimes men will go all out building stuff, or doing some "project" where they can be busy, but tears will often come at those 'safe' times. Just sitting down and crying is not normally an option for a man.

When a spouse or child dies in an accident, men will often work their grief by trying to make amends through filing law suits against the car manufacturer, or the city for having a 'dangerous intersection' etc, anything to help relieve their pain, and make them feel productive at showing how bad they feel. They want to make someone else do something to make right whatever it was that they feel caused the death. Anger, not processing.

In my Domestic Violence classes, I hear all the time that Men are Logical, Women are Emotional, and that is the way they blame their being in a DV class! If the women were just logical like men are, they claim that nothing would have happened. They remind that every time a woman wants something - she cries. Men truly believe being Stoic is a Virtue.

In readings on the subject, some biological reasons for these emotional differences do appear. Whether a man cries or does not is less important than whether he is acknowledging to himself (and if possible to another) what he is experiencing, how he is reacting and what he is doing to "work with it". Being honest with one's self is the most difficult aspect of any "problem" or situation, especially when it is dealing with loss, grief and separation.

When men are able to admit that something has changed and they are questioning "what to do about it", they are more likely to be open to suggestions, support and finding their own way. Most men don't want therapy or to be psychoanalyzed; they just want validation, acknowledgment and information. They want to feel like they're "figuring things out" on their own. Men (and women) don't need to be patronized, minimized or categorized. They want understanding, support and tools that make a difference.

Many often decide not to get involved again with someone, to avoid another loss, whether it be from death, separation or divorce. It's a fear of losing someone again. They don't want to acknowledge that man is mortal and cannot control everything, so instead of dealing with that fact, they will avoid opportunities to have to feel their mortality again!

## PRACTICAL STEPS

Of course, enjoy your trips to Starbucks, or a night out to dinner, don't isolate yourself. Reward yourself and take care of yourself as you struggle through your difficult time. GIVE YOURSELF credit for doing well! And heed what the Dalai Lama suggests...

### Dalai Lama Instructions for Life

1. Take into account that great love and great achievements involve great risk.
2. When you lose, don't lose the lesson.
3. Follow the three R's:
   Respect for self
   Respect for others and
   Responsibility for all your actions.
4. Remember that not getting what you want is sometimes a wonderful stroke of luck.
5. Learn the rules so you know how to break them properly.
6. Don't let a little dispute injure a great friendship.
7. When you realize you've made a mistake, take Immediate steps to correct it.
8. Spend some time alone every day.
9. Open your arms to change, but don't let go of your values.
10. Remember that silence is sometimes the best answer.
11. Live a good, honorable life. Then when you get older and think back, you'll be able to enjoy it a second time.
12. A loving atmosphere in your home is the foundation for your life.
13. In disagreements with loved ones, deal only with the current

situation. Don't bring up the past.

14. Share your knowledge. It's a way to achieve immortality.
15. Be gentle with the earth.
16. Once a year, go someplace you've never been before.
17. Remember that the best relationship is one in which your love for each other exceeds your need for each other.
18. Judge your success by what you had to give up in order to get it.
19. Approach love and cooking with reckless abandon.


## TUNNEL

Remember, there is an end to all this intense emotional pain. Yes, there is a light at the end of the tunnel!

When I say there is light at the end of the tunnel I am not negating the importance of your loss. I do not believe that if there is somebody very very very important in your life that you ever get over them. What I am saying is that you will get to a point where you can handle the situation and reach a balance or equilibrium of the pain versus going forward. As we have said; acceptance does not mean that you are happy about, or fine with the situation, whether it was by death or separation but it does mean that you've accepted reality and you are ready to move on.

A little further on, I will share with you an interesting article called "Dead Men in my Rolodex" because I like the context of the article which complements what I am going to say now about Quantity versus Quality of Loss which flies somewhat in the face of the way most religions and cultures deal with death. We have all heard the comment that "time heals all wounds." And most cultures and religious beliefs explain away the death of a loved one with some version of, "Sarah must've been a very special person, that God wanted her to come to heaven at such a young age." and in time you will no longer feel the pain.

In fact, I remember participating in a Grief group some years ago. A mother and daughter were part of that group. The mother had lost her son, and of course, the daughter had lost her brother, as she put it - her favorite brother. One week at the beginning of the group during what they call check-in time, the mom said, "I feel bad and I have to say that I was a bad person this week. My daughter corrected me and reminded me that God doesn't make mistakes, and that he must've really liked Jorge to have taken him at only 24 years old. My daughter reminded me that I was being selfish in expressing so much pain and anger at his loss. Jorge has gone to be a saint and I should be grateful not angry. I am sorry." She was beating herself up over her sadness. Ugh.

I personally believe that if somebody is very special in our lives we never get over them, over their deaths, over the grieving. Nor should we! Whether God took them 'because they were special', or any other way they left us, and we can rationalize their death, they are still gone. Gone. There are people I feel who'll always be with us and part of our lives even after they have died. My argument is that there is a difference between **quantity** and **quality** of grieving pain.

Yes, we all have had friends who we were very close to at some point in our lives and over time and distance they become less a part of our life to a point where we might even forget them. And with those people, there are later times in our lives when we do remember that person, that activity, or that place. Or sometimes when we are with the person again, or go to that place again, and it hits us as we think we're not sure why they were ever such a special part of our life before.

However, with somebody who is very very special, and very close to us, such as our spouse, partner, parent, child, or sibling, I feel the grieving never ever ever stops. What happens with these folks instead is that the amount of grieving becomes controllable but the intensity is still there.

For instance, when a parent loses a child there is an intensity and quantity of sadness that surrounds the parent 24/7. In time, and that time can take months, the quantity of the sadness is slowly reduced. At that point there will be times when a smile comes on the face of the parent when they are with friends or other children, there will be times when they can lose themselves in a TV show or a movie or a book, there are times when they can enjoy activities with family. However, from time to time in their lives, when that special loss hits them again about that child, the intensity or quality of the pain is just as it was the moment it happened.

Anyone who has experienced a very special loss has had that moment when weeks, months, years later they walk through the mall and ahead of them see a person or a child who looks very similar to the person they lost. And for a moment, they are taken back to the intense heavy grief of losing that person. And for a moment, they experience that entire loss again. The pain is still there and will always be. The intensity of the pain will always be the same but the amount of time feeling that pain will have lessened.

In one of my men's group sessions one day, one of the participants, Mark, gave a poignant example of the old "lemons to lemonade" story that can be applied to many things, including dealing with Grief and Loss. Mark got annoyed with someone in one of our group sessions who was whining about life and told him, "Hey, you never know what life brings, but you are responsible for your ATTITUDE and your reaction to what happens. My wife and I were expecting our first child, it was a boy. He was beautiful. I showed him around the hospital, and knew he would be everything I wasn't."

Mark continued, "He was gonna be a major league baseball player, he was gonna finish college. He was perfect. Then in time we found out something very difficult. Our only child, our boy is severely autistic. Things were gonna be different. It was like planning your life long dream vacation to the shores of South France, thinking of staying in a wonderful Villa, sipping champagne by the sea, but instead, you land in Iceland and the plane can go no further. You can adjust to the weather, the cold, and life goes on, or you moan and bitch versus make the best of what you have. New territories in your life. It's your call. We love our boy, he has taught us patience and true love. He has brought us together in ways we never would have fathomed."

Remember there are options. And you make the choice of how to handle them in most cases. For many people a life-changing situation for them has been in their careers. That can be the loss of a job due to firing, can be the loss of a job due to the company going out of business, or lately sometimes some jobs dry up due to progress. If you owned a video store in the 80s and 90s, and had progressed to DVDs in the to 2000s, you would still be 'up the creek without a paddle' today because most people do not go to brick-and-mortar stores but do their film renting or viewing via the Internet. You have the choice to become bitter or you can work at making things better and adapting to 'today'.

I am writing this now partly because many years ago something happened that stopped my progress in the agency I was working for. They had made many changes and when I applied to work my way up in the ranks there, it was made clear from members of the "old guard" that even though I was a good staff member, I would have no advancement in the agency. If I had stayed I might have reached retirement with them, gone out with the gold watch retirement gift, and been okay with it. Instead, yes, I was angry as hell in the beginning, in denial that it happened, even tried to bargain with them. Then I reached the realization that that era of my life was over. And I could either stay angry and stuck, and likely bitter, or look at other options. I ended up taking the option of moving into private practice, moving out of the county where I lived then into the city of Los Angeles, right into the middle of Beverly Hills, West Hollywood area. It is a lot harder to succeed here than in the suburbs, a lot more competition. But when I look back it was worth it.

I also had another life altering time at the end of my college years where I had planned on going into dental school and a career as a dentist. The Vietnam War and society's constant battle with the draft at that time, which took me away from being a viable college student for a while into the constant threat of being called up for war at any moment. Add to that family problems that I was in the middle of, and instead of going forward into dental school, I was blocked from that and took a temporary job teaching. That temporary job eventually, after 14 so-called temporary years, worked into a Masters degree and then Ph.D. in the field of psychotherapy. I enjoy what I do now, there are moments I have regrets that I never made it into dental school, but overall the journey has been good.

The moral of the story then, is that after we've grieved our loss, after we've been angry at what ever happened or didn't happen, the best thing is to realize this is your life, you have a limited time on this Earth, you might as well make the best of it and do something productive.

## REASON, SEASON, LIFETIME

People come into your life for a Reason, a Season, or a Lifetime. When you figure out which it is, you know exactly what to do.

When someone is in your life for a **REASON**. It is usually to meet a need you have expressed. They have come to assist you through a difficulty, to provide you with guidance and support, to aid you physically, emotionally, or spiritually. They may seem like a godsend at that point, and they are!

They are there for the reason you need them to be there. Then, without any wrongdoing on your part, or at an inconvenient time, this person will say or do something to bring the relationship to an end. Sometimes they die. Sometimes they walk away. Sometimes they act up and force you to take a stand. What we must realize is that our need has been met, our desire fulfilled, their work is done. The prayer you sent up has been answered. And now it is time to move on.

There are people who come into your life for a **SEASON**. Because it's your turn to share, grow, or learn with them. They may bring you an experience of peace, or make you laugh. They may teach you something you have never done. They usually give you an unbelievable amount of joy. Believe it! It is real! But, only for a season.

**LIFETIME** relationships teach you lifetime lessons: things you must build upon in order to have a solid emotional foundation. Your job is to accept the lesson, love the person, and put what you have learned to use in all other relationships and areas of your life. It is said that love is blind but friendship is clairvoyant.

I suggest the little book called "the Little Prince" that my friend Valentin introduced me to, there is a blurb from it in the Appendix. Read it not as a kid's book, but for the philosophy of living it presents. And, as the little Prince finds out about Life you will too. As he leaves Earth to go back to his planet, and leaves his weighty body here on earth, he tells his earthbound friend that as he looks at the lifeless shell he has left on the ground, that he really hasn't left him alone - that when the friend looks to the stars and sees them brightly shining, to realize the little Prince is there smiling brightly back at him and sending his energy. Nice thought. Take time to look at the stars and absorb their energy and beauty. They are there for YOU too, don't ignore the gifts we are given.

Dead Folks in my iPhone Contacts

Over the years we all add CONTACTS now to our phone, but back in the old days we kept business cards, or something called a Rolodex that saves business cards in it. In our lives, little by little we add new CONTACTS with phone numbers, emails, identifying facts (such as where we met them, who our mutual friends are, what their careers are) and sometimes addresses. Over the years we tend to create a long list of Contacts. Often divided into sections such as: Friends; Relatives; Business Contacts; Family.

Like so many, my CONTACTS list has grown to be intense. Sometimes when I'm looking for a phone number, I am lost in a sea of faces from the past. As I run through the list, I'll see old names, familiar names, unfamiliar names, names that bring a smile, names that bring angst. I have some well known names in there since I work with entertainment folks, some political folks, personal/mobile phones of well known folks, and some non-public numbers for access to customer service in some businesses. Often when I'm flying and heading somewhere to relax and visit, I'll get the phone out and go through my CONTACTS list as well as the photos. At that point, 35,000 feet up in the air, I try to glean out unneeded names, slimming down the CONTACTS to a more manageable level.

At those gleaning times, it always reminds me of an editorial I read years ago in a car magazine. I'm a car nerd, and the magazine editor one month did an editorial called "Dead Men in my Rolodex" which is so appropriate in a Grief and Loss book.

Here is part of that editorial:

"As I look thru my Rolodex, I see four Watanabes, and I'll be damned if I can remember one of them. Let's see: On one of the cards, I've written "short, glasses, about fifty." Oh, that helps. But I do remember the head of Mazda's Miyoshi proving ground, who gave me the card with a scratch-and-sniff banana sticker on it.

Unable or unwilling to throw a single card away, I have multiple cards with so many titles for the same guy that I couldn't tell you what he does for a living anymore, let alone where to find him. There are people in here whom I never wanted to forget (which I have), stacked up against people I hoped to never see again (which I have). I have business cards for translators, bus drivers, and limo drivers, not to mention a couple of bodyguards. Just in case.

Don't ask me where I met the director of the Kinsey Institute

67

for Research in Sex, Gender, and Reproduction or why I thought I'd need her card in the course of my daily life as an automotive journalist. Or how I came by a card from the executive director of the National Tractor Pullers Association. But can I toss it?

It occurs to me that I ought to at least throw away the "dead guys". So I steel myself and roll back cards to the A's. I'm determined to work through to Z. It's always a jolt to see that little black-and-white reminder of someone who has since passed. But what about this, right here in the As? Not a dead person, but an entire dead car company. Out comes the stack of cards from Avanti Motor Corporation, followed by a couple from the New Avanti Motor Corporation. What a shame, and let's pull these cards from the De Lorean Motor Company. And Yugo America.

That felt pretty good to do.

I shook the stained, calloused artisan hands of solid little Sergio Coggiola at the Geneva Auto Show in the 1980's. He told me then that he was worried there would be no one to carry on his work as a master model maker in Torino. May he rest in peace. This card will go

Then there are the racing drivers. The easy-laughing Jim C., who had a heart attack and died in his racing car ten years ago. Oh, and Patrick J., who died testing at Mid-Ohio, and Gordon, who died during qualifying at Indy, an hour after he'd written me a note inviting me down to hang out with his team. The great Al, who gave me the ride of my life in his Porsche in but died a few years later in a horrific plane crash.

When René D. died, I had a book he had loaned me. I sent the book to René's brother, who wrote this sad note: "Each month, receiving your magazine, René and myself enjoyed your column. Now, alone... I continue." Oh, and now, Maurice, too, has passed on. I lay their cards to the side.

This goes on through the H's and M's and to T's and see the first man I met who giggled. He hated the sound of people crunching when they ate, and we would torment him with potato chips. He died in 1992.

And there is one card I didn't expect to find – my dad's! Which settles it. I can't toss one of them. Can't even put them in a drawer to forget!

These markers for friends long gone will have a new, quiet spot of repose, but it will be in the back of the Rolodex where I can twist up my memories when I wish.

Which is as it should be - Thank you."

Keep those folks in your life that bring a Smile. Remember, I said that when a person you are close to dies, while part of you is lost and part of your life is gone with them, they in turn though, leave part of themselves with you.

When my partner died, my friend Paul had just lost his partner 6 months before. Paul was a nurse where we doctored and knew my partner well. Paul invited me to lunch so we could talk. He said, "You know, when I first lost my partner, I would rush home from work and run into our apartment. I guess part of it was because I thought maybe it wasn't true, that he hadn't died and that he might still be there waiting for me. But after a few days of course, I realized he was gone. I would still rush home and stay in our apartment for hours and hours. I didn't even answer the phone much, just sat. I didn't want to leave that energy that he had left in the apartment. I wanted to be where we had been where we cared about each other and where our relationship still had some meaning.

"I hardly went out to dinner or did anything other than go to work during the day and do errands I absolutely had to do. Then I'd run home to be in our apartment again.

"There are religions that say it takes 90 days for the dead person's spirit to leave the earth. I don't know if that's true but I can say that just about 90 days to the day after my partner died, I remember getting home and walking in the apartment where I had felt such connection with him after he died. That day I walked in, and all of a sudden a feeling of emptiness hit me. A sudden emptiness where I almost cried out, in fact, to tell you the truth I did cry out, 'Damn You, where the hell are you?' At that point I started to realize that I knew where he was. That he was now part of me. That he was with me all the time not just in the apartment anymore, but wherever I was, whatever I was doing, his spirit was with me and part of my life and would be forever.

"Jim, you will probably find that same thing happen, and I think most of us get to a point at which the person is no longer external but internal. Part of us and our daily lives."

This is where I would bring up another point. I may have or will mention this in another part of the book, but it's significant enough to say a few times. When we lose somebody through death, what we are truly left with are the memories. There's an old saying that "He who Dies with the Most Toys Wins" but toys are material things. When you look at your husband's old golf hat after he has died, or we look at grandpa's Buick LeSabre in the garage, or even look at some expensive jewelry that your wife might love to wear, the value, the dollar value, is not what brings the tears and or the ensuing smile. What brings the feelings and hopefully eventually

70

a smile to your face are those wonderful memories of that person. For that there is no dollar value.

In the movie "Meet Joe Black", which is a takeoff on an old Poem "Death Takes a Holiday" which was made into a very good movie in the 40s, we meet Death in the personification of Joe Black. To me a very significant part of the movie, is when Joe Black is visiting the emergency room of a hospital. He runs into an older Jamaican lady, who looks up at him and recognizes who he is. Since Joe Black/Death is on a holiday where he is coming to earth as a human being, to see why people are so afraid of him and to understand their feelings, there have been no deaths since he arrived for his vacation! This old lady looks up at him and very sensitively tells him she knows who he is, and she wishes he would just let her go and die. He is surprised because he has only seen people be afraid of Death up to this point. He asks her why are you willing and wanting to die? Basically she tells him that she has lived her life, it's been a good life, and that she's reached the time in her life when it's okay to say goodbye. And that she has so many wonderful memories that she will take with her into the afterlife that it will make things okay.

It's the memories... the memories...

As pointed out somewhat eloquently in "Dead Guys in my Rolodex", if somebody was very important in our lives, what's wrong with taking a moment to feel the sadness of their passing, think about them for a minute and hopefully come up with a smile of what they gave to you in their life, and to look at that memory as a Celebration of their Life.

One of my pet peeves is when people avoid talking to someone about the person in their life who has recently died. If a mother has lost a child, whether that kid was 6 or 46, people tend to talk 'around' the child, as if they never existed. I realize much of that is due to not wanting to bring up a tender subject, but the child did exist, and the pain for mom is there. The following poem eloquently addresses that situation and is worth a read from you.

## Remembering

Go ahead and mention my loved one,
The one that died, you know.
Don't worry about hurting me further.
The depth of my pain doesn't show.

Don't worry about making me cry
I'm already crying inside.
Help me to heal by releasing
The tears that I try to hide.

I'm hurt when you just keep silent,
Pretending they didn't exist,
I'd rather you mention my loved one
Knowing that they have been missed.

You asked me how I was doing
I say "pretty good" or "fine"
But healing is something ongoing
I feel it will take a lifetime.

by Elizabeth Dent

# PART THREE

# THE OLD FOLKS

The old folks don't talk much,
And they talk so slowly when they do...

They are rich, they are poor, their illusions are
gone...
They share one heart for two...
Their homes all smell of thyme,
    of old photographs and an old-fashioned song.

Though you may live in town, ... you live so far away
When you've lived too long,
    and have they laughed too much,
    do their dry voices crack, talking of times gone by
And have they cried too much,
    a tear or two still always seems to cloud the eye.

They tremble as they watch the old silver clock,
When day is through...
It tick-tocks, oh, so slow, it says, "Yes," it says, "No"
It says, "I'll wait for you."

The old folks dream no more...
The books have gone to sleep, the piano's out of tune
The little cat is dead and no more do they sing
On a Sunday afternoon...

The old folks move about no more, their world's become too small
Their bodies feel like lead... They might look out the window
    or else sit in a chair... Or else they stay in bed
And if they still go out, arm in arm, arm in arm
In the morning's chill, It's to have a good cry,
    to say their last good-bye to one who's older still...

And then they go home to the old silver clock
When day is through...
It tick-tocks, oh, so slow, it says, "Yes," it says, "No"
It says, "I'll wait for you."

The old folks never die,
They just put down their heads and go to sleep one day
They hold each other's hand like children in the dark
But one will get lost anyway
And the other will remain just sitting in that room
Which makes no sound
It doesn't matter now, the song has died away
And echoes all around

You'll see them when they walk through the sun-filled park
Where children run and play
It hurts too much to smile,
   it hurts too much but life goes on for still another day...
As they try to escape the old silver clock

When day is through
It tick-tocks oh so slow, it says, "Yes,"
   it says, "No"... It says, "I'll wait for you."
The old, old silver clock that's hanging on the wall
               That waits for us... All...
                         jacques brel

Why did I put a dreary song about Old Folks here at the beginning of the section about our FUTURES? For you to compare and realize that life is different now. If you are fortunate enough to at some point see the movie that the song came from, or catch the video on YouTube, old age is captured as tragic. But that had changed. When I went to college in 1963, we learned that the woman's lifespan had now been expanded to an average of about 68. And men were living 62 to 68. Today almost kiddingly, if somebody dies in their 70s we suggest they were too young.

When I watch the video of the old folk song it takes me back to an era when it was so true. And today it does not have to be true. In the old days, the lyrics of the song were true. The old clock was ticking and old folks knew it. Nowadays, this song doesn't ring true until much later in life, and then only if we let Father Time get hold of us. Stay alive, stay energetic, keep rollin. Listen more to Fulghum than Brel and "Live a balanced life--learn some and think some and draw and paint and sing and dance and play and work every day some."

## MOVING FORWARD

YES, the pain you are experiencing now will end! Life will go on, things will be different, but you will survive. You do have a Future. It is important to understand the process you are going through.

Now, think back to your Psychology 101 classes in High School or College. You likely heard of Kubler-Ross' and  DABDA. Dr. Kubler-Ross observed and researched folks who were dealing with terminal illnesses primarily cancer. She defined DABDA as a process of stages that people go through in dealing with terminal illnesses but, that process can be applied very well to many stages in our lives, too, and is useful in understanding many things from aging, to relationships, AND to your present loss.

D.A.B.D.A. are actually the initial letters of the

steps in Dr. Kubler-Ross' observations of how people deal with and the process of dealing with Acceptance. They stand for:

**D** enial
**A** nger
**B** argaining
**D** EPRESSION
**A** cceptance

We have all been in **DENIAL** at times in our lives. But, when we are busy denying, we don't have time to work on the real issues and we avoid seeing the real issues that need to be worked on. The blinders of **Denial** mean - No growth at that point!

When we are dealing with death it is not unusual in our pain and time of loss to not want to believe it's over. Sometimes our mind plays games on us at this point when we think we see the other person as we're walking around our home or we think we hear them in the other room. As you all know, one of the common things people say after someone dies, "I can't believe she's dead..." Of course we don't want to believe it because in the backs of our heads no matter how irrational it may be, we want to believe that the person we care about or love, will be with us forever.

In dealing with the end of the relationship, or a divorce and/or separation, it is not unusual to hear somebody say, "I can't believe she left me, what happened?" Of course the reality is in the relationships particularly the type I deal with in the Domestic Violence classes, the relationship was over a long time before it ended. We all know the situation too, where someone says to you that they are in shock about the relationship ending when they're sharing the news with you and your response is, "I'm surprised it lasted this long."

The **ANGER** stage is next. Blame, accusations. Arguing over little things that take us away from the REAL issues. It's always someone else's fault. For instance, at the END of a relationship we blame our partners, 'If only Freda would do such and such, I could have been happy,' rather than taking responsibility ourselves. When death is involved, we show Anger at GOD, "why did you take my father or mother? My child?" "I prayed that Aunt Bess would live, she was a wonderful women, and yet you let others who are less worthy live? Why? God you let me down!" Blame that leads to Anger. AND when you are Angry, you don't think clearly. No place for growth here either!

**BARGAINING** is the next step as we look at options, not always good ones, but options. Some very desperate. In relationships as it is more and more clear that the relationship is over, the couple starts to offer options to save the relationship, and BARGAIN with things like, "You can go bowling two nights a month, and I will go out with my friends two nights a month." Or, when confronted with a life threatening illness, we think lighting a few extra candles at church and bargaining with God by offering to double or triple our weekly donations - that more donations will cure us.

And with death, as we discuss, from time to time

there are left over regrets and guilt. This is a perfect time for bargaining to come in. We try to make up for what we feel we had done wrong during the relationship. We might say things like, "I'm so sorry that we didn't do this or that." Feeling guilt, sometimes we'll talk about the person to others in a super positive way, after their death, when the truth is that while they were alive we were angry with them. For instance I have a couple I worked with where the wife was coming in for counseling, and she was seriously considering divorce. She was frustrated at him for his anger issues, his seemingly lack of sensitivity toward herself and to her family, and she would discuss in sessions that she was at the end of the rope and it was over. There were weeks when they spoke very little to each other. However, when he had a sudden illness and died quickly, her comments since then have only been about how much she loved him, how great he was to her, how she thought they'd be together forever and ever. When I mentioned that she had considered divorce in the sessions, the denial jumped in, perhaps a little bargaining thrown in to make herself feel better, and she would go on about how it was my error that I had misunderstood her and that she was just 'venting' but loved him and never would leave him!!! Denial and now Bargaining with herself to make herself feel better and LESS GUILTY.

When we get to **DEPRESSION**, ahh... that most difficult word to express, particularly for men who are noted for not being emotional, and at a point at which all seems lost, when after every avenue has been pursued first in denial, then anger, trying options, blaming and then, and ONLY then, will GOOD STUFF start to happen, or at least be available to happen, when we hit the pits! Depression steps in!

At this point, we will have to think about what REALLY has happened. In bereavement groups and in my class on Loss and Grief, one of the exercises normally is: what did your family call death? What are the euphemisms you, your friends, and your family use or used for death? How comfortable are you to say, "Fred died." Instead we say things like, "My husband Fred, passed away last week." Or "My grandmother has gone to the other side." I ask people to check their feelings and see how uncomfortable they are with the words: death; died; dying.

We let our feelings come out, and start to deal with, and recognize, the reality of the situation. So **Depression** really is a good sign because NOW there is the chance we have reached a point at which we will start to work on our issues and not just blame, deny and bargain! We will start looking at the real options, and take some real action. Reading a self-help book, asking for help or guidance/counseling, recognizing something has to be done. Prayer and meditation is good at this time, because God, he or she, is silent, and lets you think things out. Meditation takes you to your center, and lets you sort things out with out criticism and arguing. Inside of you are a lot of the answers.

Now, remember, getting to **ACCEPTANCE** does not mean someone embraces and loves the results, but does mean accepting the reality of the situation. In the best case scenarios, for instance, acceptance is when a couple decides to separate and recognize they were not made for each other, and leave as friends. It's the time we realize, Grandma will not be at the table this Thanksgiving and bringing her famous pumpkin pie to share. Its time to realize 'our time together is over' as we know it today, but it does not mean that person is out of your life forever. They are part of you now, inside you, and part of your spirit. Acceptance is the point when an individual seeks help for the answers to the cause of their rage and anger. It is when a person realizes they have a life threatening disease, but they can either 'live with it', or be dying from it. Time to decide between getting Bitter, or getting Better. It is realizing your loved one has died, and that life is different now.

I remember looking at my loved one when he died, and saying out loud in the room "Ross Stewart Thayer is dead, and the team of Jim and Ross is over".

**Acceptance** is a time to look at the reality of the situation, and move forward. Not just whine or mope. And the individual starts to finally 'hear' what the reality is, and use their strengths and not just pick on everyone else's weaknesses.

Bottom line - when we reach the **Depression** stage, it is a good sign, because it means it is now time to deal with reality and not stay clouded in Anger, Denial, and desperate attempts at Bargaining, trying to save an unhealthy situation, or trying to bring back the dead, but a time to Grow and Move On by accepting reality AND living within the reality of our lives, our abilities, and our needs.

## RE-BUILD YOUR LIFE

In my book, "9 Steps to a Better LIFE", I share with readers how to make Life Happen Now for folks who are stuck and want to move forward and become the most successful productive person they can be.

The Good News is that there is hope. Re-building your Life is by definition a New Life. A little Scary? Yes. But that's okay. There are many self-help options to guide you and support you through the Journey. In my book for instance, I help guide you through what I have found to be the 9 most important steps to taking control of your life, career and future.

Some of them are presented here in this context. Create your new future, in many ways as a Celebration of the Life of the person you lost. If they were here, they would give you advice, and you can still follow that advice because you very likely knew them well enough to know exactly what they would be suggesting for you now!

## RE-PARENT YOURSELF

In dealing with Loss, you often have to recognize the emotional stuff that is holding you back and tell those inner parents to shut up while you take hold and work on things. And work on them the way YOU need it, not the way everyone is telling you. Yes, listen to suggestions, but use what works for you. As mentioned in another part of this book, men are often told to 'be a man' which normally means show no emotion, stay stoic. But you have to do what you need at the time.

Women have permission to be emotional in our culture, but some times that goes awry too. For instance, I remember my friend Pat. We were sitting having dinner in Vegas. We worked bus tours together. My partner had recently died, and I was talking and sharing with everyone about the loss when we'd be touring. She got very emotional at dinner, and started to cry. I had worked with her for a few years, and had known she was running the business by herself, and that her husband had died years before. And that was about all that was known.

That evening, as she was crying, she shared that hearing me be open about my loss, and sharing some of my emotion, that she finally felt 'safe' to share about her loss. Her husband had died eight years before! And she acknowledged that she had really not cried much nor mourned for herself. They were a busy couple, raising a few kids in the LA suburbs. He was an engineer with a small development company that he had started 15 years before. He had a staff of about 10 and worked hard putting in a lot of extra hours. Pat raised the kids, ran the home and did PTA type stuff. One morning, her husband was unusually attentive. The norm was a quick "Hi" over the newspaper and coffee, and then he'd run out the door when he realized he might be late.

That special morning, he talked for a bit about how he hadn't slept well for a number of nights due to indigestion. Then he got up to head out to the office, but came back in and kissed her good bye. Two hours later she got a call from the office that he had taken sick and was en route to the ER at the local hospital. Pat jumped in the car, and was headed toward the hospital, but said she had a funny feeling, a premonition. When she arrived at the ER, a few of the employees from her husband's company were there, and the doctor come over and said he had died of a heart attack. She cried for a few minutes, then turned to the employees there and thanked them for their help. She told me that night at dinner, she realized now that was her only 'mourning time' because she went into 'super mom' and 'super wife' mode immediately, and kept it that way til our dinner that night. For eight years, she was the super wife by going to the office, making sure it functioned the best it could without her husband's presence, and she made sure everyone got paid. After two years, she realized she would have to close the doors, since the projects he had been working on, now had been finished. He was the catalyst and instigator for projects, and now that he was gone, nothing new was happening. She shuttered the office, sent the employees off with severance packages and that era was over. She had wrapped up her duties as super-wife/boss.

With her children, she left the ER that morning, and realized she had to become the 'dad' for her son who was reaching teen years, and be there for both kids now that dad was gone. 'Super mom' did that, got them through high school, off to college and/or work and now at the dinner table that evening, she was realizing how she missed her husband, how scared she had been that she might not be able to manage on her own and how she missed her husband and his support. She cried and cried. She finally could cry about the loss and not feel guilty for taking the time out from being super-mom and super-wife to mourn her loss for herself. To take care of 'Pat'.

Loss can make your Life very confusing and difficult until you can make peace with yourself, with your inner self, become your own healthy, nurturing parent, and decide for yourself what is best. Pat had not taken care of Pat, but had taken care of every one else instead.

When you suffer a loss, put try to put yourself in the driver's seat. This is a good time to bring up something that I share with people from time to time that is meant nicely and not to be taken offensively. Many people are familiar with the term "WWJD" which means in Christian religions, when all else fails and you have to make a decision, if you're confused, you're supposed to ask yourself "What Would Jesus Do?" And as I have suggested, when you suffer a loss of a spouse, partner, parent, or close sibling, ironically the person you would normally share that pain with and look for support from, is usually the person who died. But, I also make use of that situation and recommend to others, when I get into a difficult situation where I have to make a final decision, or if I'm looking at my own life and wondering whether I'm doing the right thing or not, as we talk about in having a 'healthy inner parent', I often ask myself "WWRD". The basis of this then would be if my partner (Ross) were still alive, and I would be talking about what's going on, asking for his opinion, what would that person do and/or say? This way I can still in many ways, have his opinion because if you know somebody well, you've lived with them a long time, you know what they might say. It also is a time that allows a little bit of a smile to come over my face as I think about what my partner would have said, again with his smile and nurturing parent attitude, versus the critical parent that so many people do. So try that sometime when you are at a crossroads in trying to make a decision ask yourself "WWGD"? In this case, let the G be "What Would Grandma Do" (or say) about what I should do?

And just a reminder again, for a healthy recovery, get out of the Victim Role. We are ALL victims of Life and Death. You are not the first person to experience Loss. Move on. Take responsibility for your life, sort out your inner parent messages, toss out what doesn't work, keep what does, add some new, and become your own healthy parent championing your future.

Seek out your own truths and respect your own judgement - sometimes with that WWGD approach added in for good measure!

*This is about the Future!*
*Your Future and Life...*
***A New Beginning...***

# PART FOUR

## MANAGE DEATH and LOSSES by MANAGING LIFE GRACEFULLY

Everyone of us has to take responsibility in our lives, and for our own lives, and with that comes the responsibility of learning how to manage our lives. The good parts, the bad parts, the unfortunate things that happen, the wonderful things that happen, the abrupt changes in our lives such as an earthquake to the slow changes like aging, and the annoying things like taxes and telemarketer phone calls. And the deaths and losses in our lives too.

These are all part of our lives, and we have to learn: to sort them out, to prioritize them, to cope with them, to settle them, to deal with them and, very, very importantly, to process them. Then we have learned to Manage Life. Some folks manage life better than others, some more efficiently, some less so. Some people have great talents and have many great gifts to manage in their lives, while others have great burdens and strife to manage. Whatever the scenario, I think it is very important to learn to Manage Life with a dignity and grace, style and class. People will respect you more, you will respect yourself more.

That young man Mark I told you about earlier, who discovered his son was autistic, did not manage life gracefully at first, doing drugs and messing things up. He ended up in Domestic Violence classes over all the problems, but once he realized and accepted what life had dealt him, he became a very graceful, and grateful life manager. It can happen. Again remember,

Acceptance does NOT mean that they would choose the path of having an Autistic son but they realized the energy they were putting into drinking, drugs and anger could instead have been used to move forward and to help the kid too. With that comes growth.

You need to manage what you have to the best level you can in spite of some of the limitations, with confidence and a smile. Yes, with a smile even when it includes death - folks who have lost someone special, often have a smile come over them, when they do something that they know their deceased partner, or sibling, would kid them about if they were alive. I had one of those moments the other day when I did something sort of stupid, and I thought this would have been a time, my partner would have sat me down quietly, and gently reminded me that I was a stubborn pain in the butt! Not meanly, but in a caring way. And I smiled.

The Los Angeles County Sheriff's Academy Gun Range has posted this quote by the gun racks...

"In considering the use of deadly force, you SHALL be guided by reverence for Human Life."

This shows a respect for the fragility and vulnerability of life. The statement itself is humbling. Not a bad thought to apply to many other situations. Appreciate LIFE and LIVING. Respect Life, and those around you. Even if you are not carrying a gun, you have and can have more impact on people than you might realize.

And along that line of thinking, Agee wrote, "In every child who is born, under no matter what circumstances and of no matter what parents, the potentiality of the human race is born again, and in him, too, once more, and each of us, our terrific responsibility toward human life."

I make a trip to the Grand Canyon every few years because I love it there and it is a great place to reflect and think about LIFE and LIVING. I've hiked across the canyon - rim to rim, stayed in wilderness areas at the bottom for a week, roughed it by camping out on the rim in a tent, as well as enjoyed the luxury of the El Tovar Hotel overlooking the canyon. Enjoyed it in every way, yet it still teaches me something each and every time I go there. When I look into the canyon, and realize how magnificent it is. It humbles me to realize how insignificant I really am. I realize how immense this place is, how the power of the little water drops eroded and formed it over millions of years and, in perspective, how our short lifetimes are so insignificant in the overall picture of time and the world. How the canyon and its wildlife, from the little chipmunks who come up to visit on the rim to the birds that fly overhead to the snakes that criss cross the trails in the depths of the canyon, will all continue to go on long after I am dead and my life has ceased. And I realize and remember the canyon was able to start and form with no connection or input from me. I realize my insignificance and I get humbled.

Yet - it also gives me power as I look at its beauty and magnificence and size. And realize it is there for me (and you) to enjoy and to see. As I look at the canyon, I see how each little part of the canyon - from that little chipmunk to that snake and bird, to the drops of water in the river, all have a particular purpose in the scheme and balance of things. And they are there for me to view and share. Then, I recognize - I am significant and important, my LIFE has a meaning in the grand scheme, and then I get strength from the canyon's awesomeness. Life, yours and mine, and your neighbors, have some importance.

## DON'T BE PART OF THE PRE-DEAD

In the Disney Play, "the Lion King", the song, "The Circle of Life", has this line, "From the day we arrive on the planet, And blinking, step into the sun, There's more to be seen than can ever be seen. More to do than can ever be done." Wow, yup, even when we are offered 'more to be seen than can ever be seen', there are still plenty of bored folks all over the place. Just waiting for life to pass them by, and the end to come. Will we get to the point someday where we'll get a text saying "you're dead" in order to know?

Keep your energy going. Don't give up, use your

energy and get some support from GRIEF GROUPS, therapy, prayer, taking a walk and talking with those around you. This is where in this type of situation, we are in this together. But, don't become - ever - part of the pre-dead or Zombified folks by choice.

Remember, this is not the dress rehearsal for your REAL life. Even if you believe in re-incarnation, believing you will return again, for a second life, or a twentieth life, or whatever, if do you return, you aren't gonna have the same friends, or family, or any of the same situations you have today. Who knows, you might return as the President of the United States or as a peasant in Siberia, or even as a fly on a horse's back. Enjoy NOW for it's the only time you're gonna see today, as today!! THIS is your real life!

## ENJOY LIFE

Make the best YOU can, out of what YOU have, today, right now.  Do the best with what you have been given - your talents, your skills, your passions - NOW. Even though you have been dealt a difficult hand, play it gracefully, play it with class, play it well,  AND play it to the Max. Remember, this ain't the dress rehearsal for life, take that control you so want and deserve, don't waste it, **THIS IS YOUR LIFE**. Run with it. Run hard. And things will get better, they do. Reap the benefits of what your family and friends who have moved, died have given you as their parting gifts.

Almost 35 years ago, I wrote the following article for a local news magazine, I will share its thoughts with you here.

## APRIL FOOL

April Fool.  My life partner has AIDS. I keep waiting for somebody to come up and say,"April Fool. It's just a joke. Go ahead with your lives."  People who've lived with an AIDS patient or with other terminal diagnosis patients will understand what I'm going to say, others may find it offensive.  But, isn't it a shame that many people can't be handed a terminal diagnosis and allowed to use it to force them to sort out many of their life's problems, acknowledge what life is all about, deal with the world, come to grips with their own mortality. Find out what relationships are all about.  Find the meaning of their life. Make peace with themselves and accept themselves as whole human beings, let go of the vanity and 'super-ego' that defends them. Become the best raw loving caring best person they can be.  And then be told, "April Fool. Just Kidding.  You're fine, now use what you just learned about yourself and go forth with your long life."

For some, that period of time before they would be told "April Fool," would be days, weeks, months, and in some cases, years - depending 'how stuck' they are! What I have experienced is the amazing intensity in the life of my partner and myself as he dealt with having AIDS. Life takes on an amazing intensity when you think it is  going to end!

Though even as his medically healthy partner, I felt like we both "had AIDS" as folks dealing with cancer patients have experienced, you end up sharing the emotion and feelings on that journey. The closeness that evolved, the intensity of living, the sharing, the giving of permission to our friends to be sad about his health, to feel for their own losses in their lives. That was all shared.

Well, AIDS brought about a new intensity for living, a new spirituality to the community most hit, and it helped wipe out some of the triteness of life because - NOW - we realize every minute is a little more important in our lives.

Before my partner Ross died, we talked about a visit that was due from his mother. He felt that the visit was going to be rough, and he didn't know what he would say about his illness. He didn't know if he wanted her to visit. He said he wasn't in the mood to play "the game." I knew full well what he meant, but I played along and asked him "what game?"

He said "Well, trying to say the proper and right things in front of her. She comes from an era, and culture where you don't express feelings in public, don't say improper words, and don't cuss." You always dress for dinner, look proper, speak properly, and of course, use the salad fork only for salad and never touch anything else with it. So we talked, and he decided - sure, let her come and she has to just deal with him as he is, the way he is, and he's not going to be on guard all the time.

It's too bad, took him twenty-nine years of life to get to that point. Without AIDS he wouldn't be there now probably. Terminal illness teaches one to cut through the bullshit, and get down to the real world. Three years ago, Ross was diagnosed.  Three and a half years ago now.

In a lecture that I did for significant others of AIDS and Cancer patients, I refer to the fact that many people who live with somebody who is terminal, there's a time when you wonder how much longer it will last.  How much longer you can last or whether you are able to handle another six months or year in this situation? There is guilt that goes with that line of thought, and the reality of it, though there are times when we wonder when will it end and hope it ends soon.  I don't know how much more I can take, etc.

And those are proper feelings, and I acknowledged in the lecture that it is O.K. to think of those things as everybody does. The other side, however, it hits me that when my lover was diagnosed three and a half years ago and in the hospital, with Pneumocystis Pneumonia (an AIDS related illness) he was pretty damn sick, though he did pretty well in the first bout, it was the first time he dealt with the mortality of life.

We processed a lot of stuff out together, but six months later he was back in the hospital again with Pneumocystis. This time he had a very negative reaction to the medication. And was pretty sick.  He came out of the hospital, and ended up needing transfusions and we almost lost him.  We processed more stuff out, and did more intense thinking, and more letting go. We hit a point, when we figured it was all over. But it wasn't. Three years later, he was in the hospital again with Pneumocystis and something called CMV.  He had another rough time, and processed some more stuff out. We thought the end had arrived.

Recently, I was talking to a friend and I said, "You

know, this is draining on me, and on our friends, and I don't know that long term survival is really so good in some ways." When you lose a friend in an automobile accident who is in the prime of his life, twenty-eight or twenty-nine years old, or even the old age of forty years old, but they are healthy as can be and all of a sudden, the next morning you find out that this person is dead, there is a lot of unfinished business left.

Two years ago, a young friend of mine, a future priest, who I met when he was attending seminary, named Will, was killed in an automobile crash. I knew Will for about six years. We were close for the first couple of years, then I didn't see him for the some years. At one point, he came back into my life, and we started having some visits, we started to getting to know each other a little bit when one Halloween Evening in West Hollywood, he came up to me with some of his friends, all quite drunk and partying, he whispered in my ear, 'I really need to talk to you and Ross. I'm more sure about my life and about lots of things in my life right now and I would like to spend some time with you and Ross as soon as we can. I want to share with you, so I'll give you a call tomorrow.'

The next afternoon, I didn't hear from Will so I gave him a call. And, damn, the reason he hadn't called is that on the way home from the Halloween Party that evening he went over the side of a canyon road, and was killed instantly. A lot of unfinished business there, I always cared a lot about Will and wanted to know more about his life and apparently he had lots of things that he wanted to talk about. That was an instant sort of death. Will, I guess, was about twenty six. Very final. Very abrupt. No LONG pre-grieving and watching the person wither and fail. One day they look great and healthy, and the next day, they are gone. Dead.

The other side of the coin is the "letting go" process that happens when you have the time to do this as happens for those of us who are long time survivor AIDS Patient/Cancer Patient Survivors. We get to talk about all these things, we get to think about all these different things, and I guess we get to work all these things out. Sort of! (See the Poem in the intro, With Every GOOD BYE)

Some days it's real draining though: watching a person become so degraded by a  disease; to watch people who used to take such pride in themselves, who used to be immaculate, clean run out of energy in the shower, hate to  shower and now have to sponge bath in the sink.  I'm writing this in Martha's Vineyard on the East coast, a place where Ross liked to go as a kid with his family when he was growing up. We recently talked as he started getting very sick, and he said he would like to go to the Vineyard once more. We talked that we really shouldn't say "once more" mentality but...

So we went, and we had a bitter sweet experience for me and partly for him. The sweet part was getting on the plane that happened to serve great food, and watching him enjoy the flight and being taken care of. Watching him enjoy the food in NYC, and at the Vineyard. Watching him eat pizza at Ray's in NYC. And sitting down last night and watching him eat lobster in his favorite lobster place here.  The lobster's are caught here, and it's well known for its seafood so it's fun to watch him enjoy, that was sweet.

"The mixed grill" of emotions is riding around in the car on the island with him pointing out sights that he wants to share with me, but he is doing much from his visual memory because CMV has taken most of his eyesight. He is smiling, he is intense and enjoying sharing this special place with me. The ginger bread houses, the narrow streets and white picket fences with houses from seventeen and eighteen hundreds in Edgar Town, and Cliffs at Gay Head of Multihued Clay. He noted them very well and shared them very well with me. But it's "What's wrong with this picture?" feelings that keep hitting me. I'm seeing them and he's not - but, he is seeing it in his memory.

I'm glad for his sake that he is enjoying this trip, but I'm very sad for him and for me that he cannot see it anymore. And watching him and seeing his condition, reminds me that perhaps the end is closer as it zeros in one more time, the reality of the "letting go process."

The bitter part is sitting in the restaurant, and having to discretely direct bits of lobster closer to his fork. Maneuver his hands a little here and there so he can stick the lobster into the butter. Watching him search and yearn for the coke to drink or the napkin to wipe with. It's very degrading and humiliating situation for him as he gets frustrated, and a humbling one for me. When you look at his eyes, they look normal, but they do not see.

As I remind people who have partners who are sick that what we get down to about life, no matter how much material stuff we have accumulated, all we take with us when we die are our thoughts and memories of relationships and the people we shared our lives with. All those souvenirs we bought at Disney World or Grand Canyon they are not going with you, but the memories and thoughts are. All those things that you bought, or they bought for you, that were so special at that time, whether they were purchased at Wal-Mart, or Neiman-Marcus, they are not going to go with you. You will only pass over into that afterworld with the warm thoughts, feelings and emotions that went with those purchases of gifts.

With many terminal patients, perhaps with the indignity of being stripped of sight, of muscle tissue, of hair, of feeling and touch due to Neuropathy - this indignity and suffering actually brings a special inner strength and dignity to the person. A special insight that those who are living and doing well do not have, nor appreciate and may never acquire. A new spirituality. Yes, too bad someone has to be sick and die, to gain that knowledge and understanding. And it would be even more of a waste of a wonderful person's life if those left behind did not observe and take to heart those lessons about LIVING.

j.g. / 18 November 1992 / Martha's Vineyard

One day when I was leading my group, someone asked me how I could be cheerful and light hearted after telling over 3500 at the AIDS clinic that they likely were going to die in those early days of AIDS, and hundreds at the stroke unit, and Cancer Units, PLUS, when I worked at the school district in Thousand Oaks, somehow I got to be the one who would get the call to trot over to a school and tell a kid that their parent had died during the school day. I remember one young man, who was a 4th grader. His mom had been in an accident, she was a quadriplegic and went weekly to a place to get hydrotherapy. During the visit that week, she was left unattended for just a few minutes, and slumped over and drowned. I remember him handling my news to him better than I!

And part of the reason is not that I got jaded at dealing with death, and didn't respect it, but RATHER that I had really learned to enjoy and respect the gift of Life we have all been given. To be more at peace with myself, for as stated below, having known much sorrow, I appreciated laughter and could laugh more heartily, as well as be more tender in times of sadness.

This poem is a good wrap up for my Martha's Vineyard article -

I have known sorrow,
therefore I may laugh with you,
O Friend, more merrily than those who
never sorrowed upon earth
and know not laughter's worth...

I have known laughter,
therefore I may sorrow with you far more tenderly,
than those who never guess
how sad a thing may be.
Theodosia Garrison

The song on the following page came out during the height of the AIDS crisis, when young men in their 20 and 30's were withering to their last ounce, frail and sad, they hung in til the end. Often, as with my partner, they didn't want to go to sleep at night and would stay up til the sun came up and they realized they had made another day! They didn't want to go/die in their sleep, because they wanted that next day to happen. One time in a crowded restaurant, my partner who was getting sicker and sicker, casually said to me, "I wonder what it will be like to wake up dead?" You could hear the forks drop of the diners around us, as they grabbed the waiters and said, "We'll take this to go! NOW!"... No one likes to talk about death, or hear about it. For many, it is not a discussable topic. It was a hush hush thing.

Elton had gotten involved in the AIDS crisis by then, and offered his support. He wrote this about a person who was at that final stage - frail and near the end of their journey.

Remember, many AIDS guys were estranged from their families, and died without their support. It caught the mood, as anyone who has seen Grandma wither and die of cancer, or has watched a loved one die of any of the many illnesses that includes that horrible wasting syndrome will understand and feel the impact of these powerful and painful words.

## THE LAST SONG- Elton John

Yesterday You Came to Lift Me up
As Light as Straw and Brittle as a Bird
Today I Weigh less than a Shadow on the Wall
Just One More Whisper of a Voice Unheard

Tomorrow Leave the Windows Open
As Fear Grows Please Hold Me in Your Arms
Won't You Help Me
If You Can to Shake this Anger
I Need Your Gentle Hands to Keep Me Calm

'Cause I Never Thought I'd Lose
I Only Thought I'd Win
I Never Dreamed I'd Feel
This Fire Beneath My Skin
I Can't Believe You Love Me
I Never Thought You'd Come
I Guess I Misjudged Love
Between a Father and His Son

Things Were Never Said Come Together
The Hidden Truth No Longer Haunting Me
Tonight We Touched on the Things That Were Never Spoken
That Kind of Understanding Sets Me Free

'Cause I Never Thought I'd Lose
I Only Thought I'd Win
I Never Dreamed I'd Feel
This Fire Beneath My Skin
I Can't Believe You Love Me
I Never Thought You'd Come
I Guess I Misjudged Love
Between a Father and His Son

## THE BEST TEST OF A LIFE IS DEPTH – NOT LENGTH.

...and if Life is Depth and Intensity then:

More than fame and more than money
Is the comment kind and sunny
And the hearty warm approval of a friend;
Oh! it gives to life a savor
And strengthens those who waver
And gives one heart and courage to the end.
If one earns your praise-bestow it!
If you like him let him know it!
Let the words of true encouragement be said!
Let's not wait till life is over
And he lies beneath the clover
For he cannot read his tombstone when he's dead.

-author unknown

## DON'T LET LIFE PASS YOU BY

Here is an old Nat King Cole song that says a lot. Ironically while we are dealing with loss and grief, his funeral when he died of cancer, was one of the first 'celeb' funerals I went to.

But the words are thought provoking, and don't become the He (or she) in the song. As I watch our folks, young and old, destroy themselves and waste their time with Cocaine or stay wasted on Pot, I am sure many will be singing this song to themselves in their Senior Citizen/Golden Age years if they make it that far...

I changed the original song 'HE' to I, as I shared this with some of my druggies I've worked with to attempt to get them to think about their lives, and what they are wasting while they sit around stoned.

## Yesterday When I was Young

Yesterday When I was Young,
The taste of love was sweet as rain upon my tongue;
I teased at life as if it were a foolish game,
the way the evening breeze may tease a candle flame.
The thousand dreams I dreamed, the splendid things I
planned–
Were always built to last on weak and shifting
      sand;
I lived by night and shunned the naked light of day, And only
now I see how the years ran away.

Yesterday when I was young, so many happy songs were
waiting to be sung, so many wayward pleasures
      lay in store for me,
And so much pain my dazzled eyes refused to see.
I ran so fast that time and youth, at last, ran out.
I never stopped to think what life was all about.
      And ev'ry conversation I can now recall
Concerned itself with me, and nothing else at all.
Yesterday the moon was blue, and ev'ry crazy day
      brought something new to do.

I used my magic age as if it were a wand,
And never saw the waste and emptiness beyond.
The game of love I played with arrogance and vice. And ev'ry
flame I lit too quickly, quickly died.
The friends I made all seemed somehow to drift away... And
only I...

   am left on stage to end the play.


There are so many songs in me that won't be sung,
as I feel the bitter taste of tears upon my tongue.
The time has come for me to pay for yesterday...

   When I was young.

## AMIDST OUR LOSSES,
## KEEP YOUR INNER CHILD - ALIVE

  Hmmm, let's see: Generation Z follows Generation Y / Millennials who, as offspring of the Baby Boomers, were born 1980 to 1995. Today Millennials are 22 to 37 years old. Generation X, born 1965 to 1980, really started having more babies in 1995. Gen X offspring (Gen Z) are raised very differently than Boomer offspring (Gen Y). Are you now as confused as I am with that explanation... BUT I've said it for a reason.

  I have said numerous times, in learning about death, dealing with death, and experiencing the death of someone close to you, we learn more about Life, and about living. The following is something I wrote to a friend who is struggling in his life at the time making career choices, making some difficult personal choices after having moved away from the family in Europe. He has found things not going as well for him as his dreams had told them they would! It is a tough time for him in his life, one of those crossroads you reach where sometimes you think about "the shudda's" versus what you really want to do. His timing is during our dramas over the school shootings, the marches, the anxiety that is being caused. It is his first time in the US, and his mom warned him, "Be careful, you are young and you could get shot there." He wants to make his family happy, but when you're young, you also want to satisfy and become the best person you can be. We hear about the struggles of "the Generations". I shared him a blog to see he is not the only one struggling with direction, career and life.

"Hey Gen X, Gen Me, and Gen Z.... ,

You are in a country a bit beleaguered with some angst, anxiety and agitation. Its 4 am right now, when I'm writing this. You are prolly sleeping or studying somewhere. For an old duff like me, it's such a wonderful time to think, to work, to feel, to accomplish and create... different energy than 10 am, or 4 pm... and a weird time too, cuz its also known as "the Hour of the Wolf", (see appendix of this book), the time when most people die or commit suicide, as well as babies born. Its supposed to be a low energy time, and "safe" time for the terminally ill to let 'go' - as many of my friends, patients and my other half did. For many who have struggled for days, weeks not doing well, it is a time to say goodbye and they let go. A sad time for many, so it's also a time suicide folks decide to check out. There is no one around for them, a quiet, peaceful time, but for most an empty low energy time. The Hour of the Wolf (the hours can vary a bit) is amplified by the fact that many things look much more hopeless at 4 am, then at 4 pm when every one is around, and energy is up. And when we have friends to call, and talk to, faces to see, folks to support us.

On a whim, I went to a show a couple of years ago called "Gen Me" for the millenials. I was not expecting much, and expected to be annoyed with their attitudes about Life, about Authority and that they can all be anything they wish, values that this generation is known to expound. But I came away very moved. It was an amazing show, amazing talent (lead actor Milo and co-lead Will were amazing). As a shrink, I was glad to see that GenMe folks are humanistic enough to suffer with the Angst, Consternation, Pathos and Lament that has shaped generation after generation for a long time. It is during those times that we write our most moving, intense music, and stories and do our best art and for many thinking. I wish I had caught the show earlier, and could have seen the show again, I thank them for sharing feelings and emotions.

Grief and Loss is "the Start that we call the End". Those left behind rethink Life and carry on in the spirit of those gone. The play instead of addressing the GenMe spoiled issues that were played up so in the media - that every child needs a trophy; every child should be told they can do whatever they want in life; challenge authority because you are special; if school is tough, or you don't like your teachers, stay home and mom/dad will teach you what you need; helicopter moms who don't leave you for a minute pushing you to do your best, anything less is an unspoken failure.

BUT the play followed a different tact. It caught me off guard and my feelings that came forth as they dealt with a suicide of a seemingly well liked, successful guy student in their school. He was Prom King, and seemed destine for anything he wanted in life. And the angst that was brought about by his death by suicide, and particularly the angst and pathos his best friend went through by feeling he was "not being there" for him at a pivotal moment in the prom king's life. That suicide decision, when he was reaching out, but no one heard.

Sorry, but to be a bit more of a downer in this section, but reality sometimes is hard to deal with, we grow though from struggles and pain (No pain, no gain as your trainer at the gym says) but for instance we lost a well known comedian, Robin Williams, in 2014. It was a surprise to many, but sadly not a surprise to many others. He had made a statement that so fits in the world today too, "I used to think the worst thing in life was to end up all alone. It's not. The worst thing in life is ending up with people who make you feel alone..."

I left that play feeling there is HOPE for this generation, and the next generations thanks to some great acting by all the cast. With today's electronic music and the voice enhancers, it was a pleasure to see that some GenMe are still interested in playing real instruments. You can find a link to their trailer on YouTube.

The student rebellion that is going on following the latest Massacres due to the school shootings is another energizer. I have spent decades of my old life fighting for change, looking to leave things a little better when I expire. I have actually influenced laws in California; made changes in the law enforcement community based on community policing; helped folks in the entertainment attain things they thought were not going to happen, but I still want to do more. Watching the latest young folks is great, I tweet that while they may be the "kids of today, they ARE the adults of tomorrow". They ARE the FUTURE. I support their efforts, they will grow as they stand up to things but learning and experiencing the real world. BUT it is the child inside of us that tries new things, makes changes, enjoys life, sadly not usually the "adult".

Sitting here alone at 4 am, I am in the melancholy mind-set. I had a friend from France come visit, young wanting to model and act. I said, "I've found the Fountain of Youth", it is you and your peers such as my University students. But, too often we wait til too late to tell folks what we feel, and what they bring into our lives.

As I ruminate here, I have been looking over my 'friendship' stuff that I have been trying to share with my domestic violence/anger management group guys, guys who seem to have such adversarial lives and relationships. They have power and control issues in their lives, and even in their friendships. I ran across some things I want to share with you that I use in lectures and blogs.

"Some people come into our lives and quickly go. Some people move our souls to dance. They awaken us to new understanding, with the passing whisper of their wisdom and youth. Some people make the sky more beautiful to gaze upon and to share. They stay in our lives for awhile, leave footprints on our hearts and souls, And we are never, ... ever the same."

Gen X, Y, Z and beyond, thank you for your respect and kindness you have shown to me over the years. Folks like you give me energy, desire, purpose at 4 am to live til forever. I live off others' energy. I have many folks I see as my extended family.

Over the weekend, I lost another good friend. Ironically he was one of the ones I had given the bad news to that he had AIDS when I was working at the clinic mentioned in other places in the book. He survived longer than most. It is a haunting disease that takes lives, but being part of that generation taught us older folks a new spirituality, a spirituality that seems to take some time for the younger folks of the ME

114

generation to find. We old folks have watched our friends die, we who have been around for the last 25 years of the war on AIDS, have replaced and edited our address lists over and over as... randy, ross, billy, tony, jordy, richie, jon, mark, david, rob, geno, bob... all died too soon, all young men with futures that won't be. But we have learned the value of each person in our lives. And learned to appreciate our friends, our moments, our times. We also learned that we can't rule over our friends, control our friends, and many will just "come into our lives and quickly go, often much to quickly, but having shared the sunsets, the mountain drives, the music with them, have left that footprint in our hearts."

Over the years, I've been blessed at meeting many interesting young folks. Young people are my resource of fresh ideas, a reflection into the mirror of the world, inspiration to keep rolling, teaching, learning... and being. Interesting, unique folks, some are the servers who have made my lunches and dinners in restaurants more interesting. I gotta tell you, don't lose that energy, passion, enthusiasm drive, wonderment and awe that you show no matter how difficult things can be as the young folks who have been in the schools and places where many of their friends have been lost. In this world there are the Movers, the Shakers, and the Followers. Sort of like a colony of bees with its drones, the workers, the Queens, (no offense meant about Queens!!). Some people are here to set a pace for others to follow. Some of us are creative and given the special-purpose to FORM the "tomorrows" that we all will experience.

Others are given a special-purpose, or job, to make sure that "tomorrow" just happens. They are the dependable, conforming, efficient workers and drones. But, we, people like you and me, do the thinking, probing mostly because we retain our child inside of us - forever. Our inner child is nurtured forever by wonderment and awe, and we must forever nurture and care for that child who is the foundation of us. We are often told to "grow up, you aren't a kid anymore", but we started the foundation of our lives as a child. If we took away the foundation and first 12 floors of the Empire State building in NYC, and moved it away, but still wanted to have the upper floors, what would happen to the building? It would crumble and look like so many sad and lost and unhappy folks we meet everyday! Their child is gone, dead inside of them. Non-existent. Many do not look around in awe and wonderment, but just exist. Do not lose that ability. Many years ago the earliest reading books started with simple stories, and words "Look. Look. See. See Spot run. Look at Spot run." we learned to read with simple words, but with important words. **LOOK. SEE. HEAR. LISTEN**.

The conformers/workers are the adults who look at a glass and see a glass. They look at a tree and see a tree. They look at a house and see a house. They make sure that the glass is filled at the restaurant, that the tree gets taken care of and fed, pruned and that it will be there for our children tomorrow, they take the house and make sure it's an efficient and comfortable home for their families, for their children of tomorrow. WE do need them. But, the creative one looks at the damn tree - not myopically, but with 'vision', dreams - thinking "wow, what a beautiful tree, what intricacies, what depth to it". I look at the tree and I think of what beauty nature has to offer, the fascination that this damn tree will still be here when I croak, and God knows how long that tree's been here before I came on the scene, and where in the hell did it come from, or who the hell planted it? I think of the connection with nature and how the universe just plain functions, how nature provides for itself, in spite of us. How awesome. I worry that the tree won't get cut down and worry about how we abuse nature, where we are it's

116

"guests", and often not very responsible guests.

I look at my house not just as brick and mortar that meets my needs, but I look at my house as a home that provides me a nurturing environment, that recharges my batteries, rejuvenating, that gives me the energies that I need to go out and face the next day, and provides my shelter. It makes me feel good, it expresses me, it shows "Me". When people come into my home they get to know me, my likes, my desires, my wants, maybe even my fears just by what I have in my home. Its an expression, it's my canvas.

This leads me to that bit of spirituality where I realize I am part of the world, part of an exciting place and I want to see more, want to do more, I think of the tree as an expression of myself with the branches that keep reaching out, and up. I wonder to myself what I can do and where I can go and what I haven't explored yet and where the branches might take me, as well as think of my roots - my legacy is what I am sowing everyday. The students I teach, the folks I visit with, are part of that legacy.

Remember, the wonderful emotion and feelings that come out when young folks talk about things. That's so cool. Don't lose that energy, just don't. Don't lose that child inside of you, the child that provides, gives, thrives on wonderment and awe, the child that IS wonderment and awe. Nurture your child, and heal the hurt kid that still is in there. - the little kid that still hurts at times. And for those of you who have already lost friends, feel as sad as you need to, miss them, love them and do them honor as you are the FUTURE, not just FUTURE adults, but THE FUTURE. It's yours, you'll do fine, yup, you will.

Sincerely, your really OLD friend - dr. jim

I have said numerous times, in learning about death, dealing with death, and experiencing the death of someone close, we learn more about life, and about living. The following is something I wrote to a friend to help him as he was struggling in his life at the time making career choices, making some difficult personal choices after having moved away from the family back in the Midwest and coming out to do his "own thing" against the family's wishes, and having found things not going as well for him as his dreams had told them they would. It was a tough time for him in his life, one of those crossroads you reach where sometimes you think about "the shudda's" versus what you really want to do. There is some guilt and frustration because you think of wanting to make your family happy, but you're young and you also want to satisfy and become the best person you can be.

## HERE ARE SOME THINGS TO CONSIDER IN HELPING SOMEONE WHO HAS LOST SOMEONE

Many of the points in the following Hospital In-service I did for my Staff at the Stroke and Rehab Unit are good points to ponder. The staff (nurses, aides, Occupational Therapists, Speech Therapists, Physical Therapists) had all come from an Acute Care setting to the Long Term Care with Stroke and Eldercare Re-hab patients. A very different situation. Prior to working that unit, I had not really thought about those differences myself, and had to do research to understand the difference, and what was needed.

### From Dr. Jim's STAFF IN-SERVICE
### re: Acute vs. Long-term Care

1. DABDA. Good old Kubler-Ross's defined process of dealing with loss. Denial, anger, bargaining, depression, acceptance. Denial is more than a river in EGYPT! With your patients, for YOU, it's dealing with and accepting loss of their abilities, facing mortality (yours and theirs), recognizing the loss of some future goals or at least redefining their future for them, and facing Reality. ACCEPTANCE, does not mean defeat, but recognizing reality and adjusting future goals and plans so the person can LIVE to their fullest!

2. These patients are re-defining their lives, their relationships, their futures. In fact, due to one catastrophic or traumatic incident, a moment in their

daily lives, their whole life has been re-defined for them! Consider your role in facilitating their acceptance of, and understanding of that change and process.

3. All patients need to be "allowed" (and in many times encouraged) to process out their losses, to grieve, talk out their sadness, fears, anger... and then be ready to move on... And become healthy again even if in a lesser body.

4. Trauma such as having a stroke are a "shock" into reality. Something that is a reality and possibility in life, that many folks haven't dealt with while healthy, so they are going to have even a harder time with reality now. Recognizing mortality can be difficult. Remember, illnesses and crisis AMPLIFY a person's psychological pathology. So, if they were aggressive and angry before the stroke, they are likely to be more so now!. If they tended to be depressed before the stroke, they might be even more so now.

5. The patient's reality base has changed, things MAY seem insurmountable at this time, AND some things will be insurmountable permanently. They should be allowed to have a short pity party, and even return to it later if they need to but your responsibility is somewhat like a ship's purser, to let them enjoy their party, yet guide them toward a safe and happy journey that is productive to them.

6. There is a traumatic impact to the changes in their bodies and lives, and the after effects they have to deal with. Think of how you might handle one day being

fully capable and productive, and then waking up the next day unable to toilet yourself. You too have the right to feelings. "Being strong" does not mean having no feelings. For you as a staff, it is being strong enough to help them sort things, and give them the support they need in becoming the best they can be now. Remember, you are a human being and probably cannot restore them to full abilities, but you can do the best you can be to help them achieve their best. AND you will have to also acknowledge your feelings as they come up.

7. There are differing reactions in care- givers who work with patients who suffer strokes and long lasting illness. Transference (*see Glossary) and Counter-transference issues can become an issue for the care-giver of re-hab patients. In dealing with Acute Care patients, who are usually short term, your personal feeling will have less time to build, there will be less time to connect. In a Re-hab Center you get closer, more involved with the patient and their lives often even making home visits to prepare for their move back home and then you see more of their personal life then you ever did with acute care patients. Plus you get closer to their families. CAUTION: do not become an accidental Enabler. ALLOW patients to do for themselves - no matter how slow they are, nor how much more expedient it might be for you to do it yourself. AND medication should not be used to suppress their need to cry, mourn their loss, and move on. Nor used to suppress the feelings they should have. Feeling bad, sad, angry IS part of the recovery process.

8. Remember: re-hab patients can and do push

the "loss of control of our lives" and aging buttons in staffers themselves, as you internally think, "will I be in this state and condition some time?"

9. The following is a poem originally written as the "Portrait of a Friend" but in it, I remind you as a staff, and my college students who are going into the Mental Health field and are going to be caretakers of some sort, that they can only do so much. The following is that poem modified for the people going into the 'helping' field:

### "Portrait of a Therapist/Caretaker"

I can't give solutions to all of life's problems, doubts, or fears. But I can listen to you, and together we will search for answers.
I can't change your past with all it's heartache and pain, nor the future with its untold stories.
But I can be there now when you need me to care.

I can't keep your feet from stumbling.
I can only offer my hand that you may grasp it and not fall.
Your joys, triumphs, successes, and happiness are not mine; yet I can share in your laughter.

Your decisions in life are not mine to make, nor to judge; I can only support you, encourage you, and help you when you ask.
I can't prevent you from falling away from our therapy, or from your personal values. I can only guide you, talk to you and wait for you to grow.

I can't give you boundaries which I have determined for you, but I can give you the room to change, room to grow, room to be yourself.

I can't keep your heart from breaking and hurting. But I can sit and support you and help you pick up the pieces and put them back in place.

I can't tell you who you are. I can only be your sensitive listening ear. And help you find who you are.

–Dr. G.

## AGING BEATS THE ALTERNATIVE

Recognizing that others have thoughts about Loss, Grief and even the Aging process that leads to that Loss and Grief, helps us realize our feelings are not unfounded. Our fear and/or concern of getting to the end is not abnormal, we are not alone. Tonight I spoke with a young man in his 20s who expressed that he has been obsessed with fear of his death, and his unique response was that he hoped he died young so that he didn't have to continue having difficult nights of thinking about death. Sort of a 'let's get it over with' routine. He lives the days very intensely trying to enjoy everything, then sadly goes to bed afraid.

Here is one of those internet gems that rings true in so many ways as the writer talks about Life and its value. The fact that friends have a purpose, and that support is needed for all of us.

"I would never trade my amazing friends, my wonderful life, my loving family for less gray hair or a flatter belly. As I've aged, I've become kinder to myself, and less critical of myself. I've become my own friend. I don't chide myself for eating that extra cookie, or for not making my bed, or for buying that silly cement gecko that I didn't need, but looks so avant garde on my patio. I am entitled to a treat, to be messy, to be extravagant.

"I have seen too many dear friends leave this world too soon; before they understood the great freedom that comes with aging.

"Whose business is it if I choose to read or play on the computer until 4 AM and sleep until noon? I will dance with myself to those wonderful tunes of the 60 &70's, and if I, at the same time, wish to weep over a lost love... I will.

"I will walk the beach in a swim suit that is stretched over a bulging body, and will dive into the waves with abandon if I choose to, despite the pitying glances from the jet set.

"They, too, will get old. I know I am sometimes forgetful. But there again, some of life is just as well forgotten. And I eventually remember the important things.

"Sure, over the years my heart has been broken. How can your heart not break when you lose a loved one, or when a child suffers, or even when somebody's beloved pet gets hit by a car? But broken hearts are what give us strength and understanding and compassion. A heart never broken is pristine and sterile and will never know the joy of being imperfect.

"I am so blessed to have lived long enough to have my hair turning gray, and to have my youthful laughs be forever etched into deep grooves on my face.

"So many have never laughed, and so many have died before their hair could turn silver. As you get older, it is easier to be positive. You care less about what other people think. I don't question myself anymore. I've even earned the right to be wrong.

"So, to answer your question, I like being old. It has set me free. I like the person I have become. I am not going to live forever, but while I am still here, I will not waste time lamenting what could have been, or worrying about what will be. And I shall eat dessert every single day(if I feel like it).

"MAY OUR FRIENDSHIP NEVER COME APART ESPECIALLY WHEN IT'S STRAIGHT FROM THE HEART! MAY YOU ALWAYS HAVE A RAINBOW OF SMILES ON YOUR FACE AND IN YOUR HEART FOREVER AND EVER! FRIENDS FOREVER!"....... *SueAnne*

# IT'S A WRAP

I live and practice in the film and entertainment capital of the World, so as they say when they finish filming movie or winding up a night of a TV taping - "It's a Wrap." We are at the end of the book and our time together. A few years ago, I wrote a blog, that I will share here as part of 'my wrap.'

Finding about ourselves is a difficult journey, sometimes painful, and some never get 'there', but it can be wonderful in its own way. I'm sure you've heard the phrase psychological writers and 12 steppers toss about - "the Journey to Self." I have shared a lot of that with you in this book, and it fits so, so much in this context.

Our journey, our life... In that blog I shared about my partner Ross' dying in 1993 - when Ross died, he didn't 'pass on', 'go to sleep', or any other euphemism - he died and passed over into whatever that is we go to after we die. That morning, I turned to him, and looked at him that 4:44 am, January 28th, 1993, and I realized he was now dead on our bed. His body was cooling off, I saw that Life was going out of him. He was slumped over, his journey was done... Our journey together as we knew it was over. As I shared earlier, I actually said out loud, "This is the end of Ross Stewart Thayer, and the team of Jim and Ross", at least as it had existed for many years.

So often before, when we traveled around the country, on that same bed he died in, is where we would place our bags to be packed for the next trip, or journey. It was a convenient place to pack them. When we traveled, we mostly used soft black leather duffles. As we placed them on the bed to pack, they would be limp and slumped. But as we filled them up for our journey, they took a shape, they had a purpose - almost like a personality. They took on positive feelings about them as we would talk about what we were going to take, and what we might need on the trip. Swimsuits, cameras, maps, daily clothes.

At the end of our trip, we would place those same bags back on that bed to unpack. Removing the things from the trip, from that journey. The things that made it a journey from the dirty laundry, to the extra clothes, to the things we had taken to read, to the used airline ticket stubs, and the mementos of the trip we had picked up along the way.

As we unloaded them, the bags would start to sag and slump, and sadly, it was a sign that journey was over. But we knew the memories we made during the trip, the journey, were still with us, and would be for the rest of our lives.

As Ross slumped in the bed, and his journey on this earth was over, as our lives together ended, he reminded me of those empty travel duffles. They had served us well, as had his body, but he didn't need it anymore. And from then on he would be part of my life, and part of me, internally, as a memory, a legacy. And his impact on me affects all those who I deal with everyday.

The memories are what we have, the memories are what make our journey worth it. Memories are what make a relationship, a friendship, a LIFE. Pets are a great example, your pet hamster, your cat, and your dog all will have a shorter life span than you, and they will die...

But their time with you should give some great memories for you, and they should have a wonderful time with you, playing and enjoying your love and affection. And they too will help you have memories.

Make your Journey productive. Leave a legacy, impact many around you, and those who come after you. Too often someone says, 'If I can just help one person, I've done well', nope - that would be a waste of your talents, spread good things, teach many to sing, to dance, to enjoy, or even just to LOOK. Awe and wonder is the parent of the child inside of all of us, and the child is what keeps us humming... and singing... and dancing, when the adult in us is telling us NO. Listen to your kid.

Use your talent. Make your journey worth it.

dr. g., 2021

# ADDENDUM

**All I Really Need to Know I Learned in Kindergarten**

All I really need to know about how to live and what to do and how to be I learned in kindergarten. Wisdom was not at the top of the graduate school mountain, but there in the sandpile at Sunday School.

These are the things I learned:
Share everything. Play fair.
Don't hit people. Put things back where you found them.
Clean up your own mess. Don't take things that aren't yours.
Say you're sorry when you hurt somebody.
Wash your hands before you eat.
Flush.

Warm cookies and cold milk are good for you.
Live a balanced life – learn some and think some and draw and paint and sing and dance and play and work every day some.

Take a nap every afternoon.
When you go out into the world, watch out for traffic,
hold hands, and stick together.

Be aware of wonder. Remember the little seed in the Styrofoam cup: The roots go down and the plant goes
up and nobody really knows how or why,
but we are all like that.

Goldfish and hamsters and white mice and even the little seed in the Styrofoam cup--they all die.

So do we.

And then remember the Dick-and-Jane books and the first word you learned--the biggest word of all--LOOK.

Everything you need to know is in there somewhere. The Golden Rule and love and basic sanitation. Ecology and politics and equality and sane living.

Take any one of those items and extrapolate it into sophisticated adult terms and apply it to your family life or your work or your government or your world and it holds true and clear and firm.

Think what a better world it would be if we all--the whole world--had cookies and milk about three o'clock every afternoon and then lay down with our blankies for a nap.
Or if all governments had as a basic policy to always put things back where they found them and to clean up their own mess.

And it is still true, no matter how old you are-- when you go out into the world, it is best to hold hands and stick together.

--Robert Fulghum

## Let Me Go

When I come at last to the end of the road,
And the sun has set for me,
I want no rites in a gloom-filled room.

Why cry for a soul set free?
Miss me a little, but not too long.
And not with your head bowed low.

Remember the love that we have shared.
Miss me - but let me go.

For this is a journey we all must take,
And each must go alone.
It's a part of the master plan.
A step on the road to home.

When you are lonely and sick at heart,
Go to the ocean we know.
And bury your sorrow among the waves,
miss me -

... but let me go,
thank you.

## PRAISE NOW

If with pleasure you are viewing
Any work a man is doing
And you like him or you love him,
say it NOW!

Don't withhold your approbation
Till the parson makes oration
And he lies with snowy lilies o'er his brow.
For no matter how you shout it
He won't really care about it

If you think some praise is due him
Now's the time to hand it to him
For he cannot read his tombstone
when he's dead!

And here is a sobering thought...
that has popped up on the internet...
Is this what Death is?
In Death, do we just exist in a dreamworld?
Someday, we'll know...

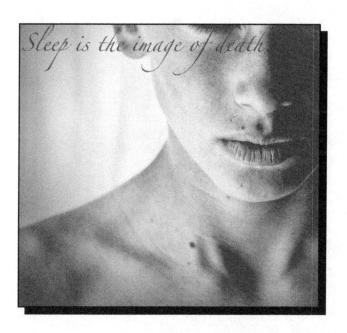

# THE HOUR OF THE WOLF

In the hour of the wolf which is the time of midnight
sun and midday moon, there are questions.
At the hour of the wolf, the dark hearts hin
and the pure hearts quail,
and the questions still remain

At the hour of the wolf,
that which was immutable is insubstantial
and that which was smoke and shadow responds to
your touch, and the questions become
insistent

Upon the hour of the wolf,
Hours last for minutes, and minutes last for seconds,
and seconds last forever,
and there are questions

When it's the hour of the wolf,
You'll punish yourself, praise yourself.
You'll love and hate yourself.
Cry about what you did right,
rejoice about what you did wrong.
And you'll ask yourself who am I, why am I, and
what's the point.

After the hour of the wolf, You'll know who you are,
why you are, and what the point is.
But you'll be alone...
And alone, you'll never recognize your answers.
And you'll never leave... the hour of the wolf.

## AND... "The Little Prince" puts it in perspective...

If you haven't read the book (it's available on Amazon and other sources- please buy it, read it!) or don't know the story -

So it goes: Many years ago, a military pilot crash lands in the desert, his old prop style plane is majorly damaged, he is alone and thinks he will die... alone. At one point, a young boy shows up who claims to be a Little Prince from a far away little planet. They become fast friends, spending lots of time together. And thanks to the Little Prince's 'presence', inner peace and support, the pilot finds the energy, and drive, to fix his plane so he can eventually return home. During their time together the Little Prince talks a LOT - a whole lot - jabbering wisdoms beyond his age, and telling the pilot about what he has learned about Human-kind and Life as he had visited other planets before he came to planet Earth to visit.

At the end of his year on Earth, where he is now hanging out with the Pilot in the desert, he realizes his 'Journey on Earth' is done, and its time to go 'back to his planet'. I present the last two short chapters where the Little Prince dialogues with the pilot as he plans to 'take leave of Earth, and his earthly body' and return to his planet faraway. They are presented with some minor modifications. And as you read the chapters, remember, the Little Prince believed that only children could understand Life, and only children would be interested in what made Life...Life. He felt that adults were too stuck in their ways, and too focused on their own lives to learn about LIFE. Most adults will not 'get' the story of the Little Prince and his message, but remember, the 'child' inside of us is nurtured by awe and wonder, it is what makes life worth living. Keep that child inside of you - nurture it, and you will stay young.

I have taken the Little Prince's advice myself, and I go up to our roof patio overlooking the Los Angeles Basin, and look at the stars often. From the rooftop, I look at the millions of people around me in Los Angeles, knowing that even in the middle of such an over-crowded area, there are still people dying of loneliness and unhappiness. And that most never look up at the stars, or the moon, or the clouds, or watch a sunrise or sunset for solace and comfort, nor do they hear the laughter and energy I get from those stars as I talk to friends and family who have departed whether it by death, or just distance. There are so many wonderful gifts people don't allow into their lives. Take the time to look around, and enjoy this life, it is YOURS, and do enjoy this blurb from the Little Prince.

dr. g.

---

## Chapter 26

Beside the water well there was the ruin of an old stone wall. When I came back from my work on the plane, the next evening, I saw from some distance away my little prince sitting on top of a wall, with his feet dangling. And I heard him say to something below the wall: "Then you don't remember. This is not the exact spot."

Another voice must have answered him, for he replied to it: "Yes, yes! It is the right day, but this is not the place."

I continued my walk toward the wall. At no time did I see or hear anyone.

The little prince, however, replied once again: "Exactly. You will see where my track begins, in the sand. You have nothing to do but wait for me there. I shall be there tonight."

I was only twenty metres from the wall, and I still saw nothing.

After a silence the little prince spoke again: "You have good poison? You are sure that it will not make me suffer too long?"

I stopped in my tracks, my heart torn asunder; but still I did not understand.

"Now go away," said the little prince. "I want to get down from the wall."

I dropped my eyes then, to the foot of the wall– and I leaped into the air.

There before me, facing the little prince, was one of those yellow snakes that take just thirty seconds to bring your life to an end. Even as I was digging into my pocket to get out my revolver, I made a running step back. But, at the noises I made, the snake let himself flow easily across the sand like the dying spray of a fountain, and, in no apparent hurry, disappeared, with a light metallic sound, among the stones. I reached the wall just in time to catch my little man in my arms; his face was white as snow.

"What does this mean?" I demanded of him. "Why are you talking with snakes?"

I had loosened the golden muffler that he always wore around his little neck. I had moistened his temples, and had given him some water to drink. And now I did not dare ask him any more questions, I knew he never liked questions, nor ever really answered them except with more of his own questions about Life. He looked at me very gravely, and put his arms around my neck. I felt his heart beating like the heart of a dying bird, that had been shot with someone's rifle...

"I am glad that you have found what was the matter with your airplane engine," he said. "Now you can go fly again and go back home–"

"How do you know about that?" for I was just coming to tell him that my work had been successful, beyond anything that I had dared to hope. He made no answer to my question, but he added: "I, too, am going... back home today..."

Then, sadly, I said– "It is much farther to your planet than my home... it is much more difficult..."

I realized clearly that something extraordinary was happening. I was holding him close in my arms as if he were a little child; and yet it seemed to me that he was rushing headlong toward an abyss from which I could do nothing to restrain him... His look was very serious, like someone lost far away. He was... leaving me.

And he gave me a sad smile. I waited a long time. I could see that he was reviving little by little.

"Dear little man," I said to him, "I know you are afraid..." He was afraid, there was no doubt about that. But he laughed lightly.

"I shall be much more afraid this evening..."

Once again I felt myself frozen by the sense of something irreparable. And I knew that I could not bear the thought of never hearing his laughter any more. For me, it was like a spring of fresh water in the desert.

"Little man," I said, "I want to hear you laugh again."

But he said to me: "Tonight, it will be a year... my star, my planet, then, can be found right above the place where I came to the Earth, a year ago... I have to go."

"Little man," I said, "tell me that it is only a bad dream– this affair of the snake, and the meeting-place, and the star... of you leaving."

But he did not answer my plea. He said to me, instead: "The thing that is important is the thing that is NOT seen..."

"Yes, I know..."

"It is just as it is with the flower. If you love a flower that lives on a star (the Little Prince often talked about his Rose that he cared for on the little planet/star he came from and how special that Rose was, it was only one Rose, but it was his Rose, and he had to care for it), it is sweet to look at the sky at night. All the stars are a-bloom with flowers..."

"Yes, I know..."

"It is just as it is with the water. Because of the pulley, and the rope at the well that you gave me a drink that was like music. You remember– how good it was."

"Yes, I know..."

"And from now on, at night you will look up at the stars. Where I live everything is so small that I cannot show you where my star is to be found. It is better, like that. My star will just be one of the stars, for you to look at. And so you will love to watch all the stars in the heavens... they will all be your friends. And, besides, I am going to make you a present now..."

He laughed again.

"Ah, little prince, dear little prince! I love to hear that laughter!"

"That... that is my present. Just that. It will be as it was when we drank the water at the well and were happy... and laughed together."

"What are you trying to say?"

"All men have the stars," he answered, "but they are not the same things for different people. For some, who are travelers, the stars are guides. For others they are no more than little lights in the sky. For others, who are scholars, they are problems. But all these stars are silent. You– you alone– will have the stars as no one else has them–"

"What are you trying to say?"

"In one of the stars I shall be living. In one of them I shall be laughing. And so it will be as if all the stars were laughing, when you look at the sky at night... you– only you– will have stars that can laugh!"

And he laughed again.

"And when your sorrow is comforted (time soothes all sorrows) you will be content that you have known me. You will always be my friend. You will want to laugh with me. And you will sometimes open your window, so, for that pleasure... and your friends will be properly astonished to see you laughing as you look up at the sky! Then you will say to them, 'Yes, the stars always make me laugh!' And they will think you are crazy. It will be a very shabby trick that I shall have played on you..."

And he laughed again.

"It will be as if, in place of the stars, I had given you a great number of little bells that knew how to laugh..."

And he laughed again. Then he quickly became

serious: "Tonight– you know... do not come here," said the little prince.

"I shall not leave you," I said.

"I shall look as if I were suffering. I shall look a little as if I were dying. It is like that. Do not come to see that. It is not worth the trouble... Stay with your plane, and get ready to fly home."

"I shall not leave you."

But he was worried. "I tell you– it is also because of the snake. He must not bite you. Snakes– they are malicious creatures. This one might bite you just for fun... Stay with your plane and get ready to fly home. You must."

"I shall not leave you."

But a thought came to reassure him: "It is true that they have no more poison for a second bite. So I could not be bitten."

That night I did not see him set out on his way. He got away from me without making a sound. When I succeeded in catching up with him he was walking along with a quick and resolute step. He said to me merely: "Ah! You are there..."

And he took me by the hand. But he was still worrying. "It was wrong of you to come with me. You will suffer. I shall look as if I were dead; and that will not be true..."

I said nothing.

"You understand... it is too far to my star. I cannot carry this body with me. It is too heavy."

I said nothing.

"But it will be like an old abandoned shell. There is nothing sad about old shells..."

I said nothing.

He was a little discouraged. But he made one more effort: "You know, it will be very nice. I, too, shall look at the stars. All the stars will be water wells with a rusty pulley. All the stars will pour out fresh water for me to drink and

140

rejoice...as you and I did once when we were desperate for water and found the well."

I said nothing.

"That will be so amusing! You will have five hundred million little bells in the sky to look at... and I shall have five hundred million springs of fresh water..."

And he too said nothing more, because he was crying... "Here is the place... Let me go on by myself."

And he sat down, because he was afraid. Then he said, again: "You know— my flower... I am responsible for her on my star. And she is so weak! She is so naive! She has four thorns, of no use at all, to protect herself against all the world... I have to go and take care of her."

I too sat down, because I was not able to stand up any longer.

"There now— that is all..."

He still hesitated a little; then he got up. He took one step. I could not move.

There was nothing but a flash of yellow close to his ankle. He remained motionless for an instant. He did not cry out. He fell as gently as a tree falls.

There was not even any sound, because of the desert sand.

## Chapter 27

And now six years have already gone by since that night... I have never yet told this story. The companions who met me on my return were well content to see me alive and back from the crash site. I was sad, but I told them: "I am tired."

Now my sorrow is comforted a little. That is to say— not entirely. But I know that he did go back to his planet, because I did not find his body at daybreak. It was not such a heavy body, he was a little prince ... and at night I love to listen to the stars. It is like five hundred million little bells...

But there is one extraordinary thing... now I keep wondering: what is happening on his planet? At one time I say to myself: "Surely the little prince puts his flower under her glass globe every night, and he watches over his sheep very carefully... and all is well on that planet." Then I am happy. And there is sweetness in the laughter of all the stars.

But at another time I say to myself: "What if something went wrong on the planet... and...?" And then the little bells are changed to tears...

For you who also love the Little Prince, and for me: Look up at the sky. Ask yourselves what is important in life. And you will see how everything changes...

And no grown-up will ever understand that this is a matter of so much importance!

This is, to me, the loveliest and saddest landscape in the world - think of that place in the desert where that the little prince appeared on Earth, and disappeared.

In case you travel some day to the African desert. And, if you should come upon that spot, please do not hurry on. Wait for a time, exactly under the star. Then, if a little man appears who laughs, who has golden hair and who refuses to answer questions, you will know who he is. If this should happen, please comfort me. Send me word that he has come back. In the meantime, look at the stars where you are, talk to them, and listen to their laughter...

**They are there for YOU**.

# GLOSSARY

**angst** - German word, an acute but nonspecific sense of anxiety or remorse, in Existentialist philosophy it's the dread caused by man's awareness that his future is not determined but must be freely chosen

**clinical depression** - a more severe, persistent form of depression. Signs and symptoms may include: loss of interest in daily activities; persistent sadness or feeling of emptiness; sleep disturbances; significant weight loss or gain; loss of concentration; fatigue; suicidal thoughts or behavior.

**consternation** - A state of paralyzing dismay. A feeling of anxiety, dread, or confusion.

**counter-transference**- The caretakers projection on to the client of emotions which originate in their own personal life or history.

**EOL** - End of Life, 'that time... as we say goodbye....

**Hour of the wolf** -
http://www.bhcounseling.com/articlespoems06.html

**humbleness** - not proud or arrogant; modest: *to be humble although successful.* courteously respectful, *In my humble opinion you are wrong.*

**humility -** the defining characteristic of an unpretentious and modest person, someone who does not think that he or she is better or more important than others; can be confident, but is not arrogant, *Gandhi, Jesus, Martin Luther King, jr., the Dalai*

*Lama would all be described as showing humility.*

**lament -** v. To express grief for or about; mourn as in lament a death. To regret deeply; deplore. To grieve audibly, wail and to express sorrow. n. A feeling or an expression of grief; a lamentation. A song or poem expressing deep grief or mourning

**pathos -** the quality or power, especially in literature or speech, of arousing feelings of pity, sorrow, etc., a feeling of sympathy or pity.

**transference -** The process by which patients identify the caretaker with important people in their lives, usually their parents or children, and project on the caretaker their relationship with those people.

**AND Special Thanks to:**
Abdelaziz, Beckie, Carol,
Cathy, Christy, Fred, Georgia,
Janette, Josiah, Matt, Mimi,
and Sergey Valentin

RIP: Aunt Helen, Aunt Lil,
Shirley Hudson, Rod McKuen,
&
the wonderful gentle soul
who I owe so much to -
Ross Stewart Thayer